Outstanding Books for the College Bound

Choices for a Generation

Marjorie Lewis

Editor

American Library Association
Chicago and London 1996

Cover design by Richmond Jones

Text design by Dianne M. Rooney

Composed by Graphic Composition in Optima and Melior
on the Miles system

Printed on 50-pound Hospitality Opaque paper, a pH-
neutral stock, and bound in 10-point C1S cover stock
by Victor Graphics, Inc.

The paper used in this publication meets the minimum
requirements of American National Standard for Information
Sciences—Permanence of Paper for Printed Library
Materials, ANSI Z39.48-1992.⊗

Library of Congress Cataloging-in-Publication Data

Outstanding books for the college bound : choices for a
  generation / Young Adult Library Services Association ;
  Marjorie Lewis, editor.
        p.   cm.
    Includes index.
    ISBN 0-8389-3456-0
    1. College students—United States—Books and
  reading.   2. Best books.   I. Lewis, Marjorie.   II. Young
  Adult Library Services Association.
  Z1039.C6509   1996
  011.62′5—dc20   96-5086

Printed in the United States of America

00 99 98 97 96   5 4 3 2 1

CONTENTS

PREFACE

Once, when I was younger, gathering credits for school certification, I asked the professor (who was head of the English department at a prestigious public school) why there seemed to be a universal core of literature taught at specific grade levels that never seemed to change. I remarked that the literature taught was the same wherever I had lived, in Ohio, New York, New Jersey, and London. He acknowledged the truth of this and observed that it was true wherever schools were preparing students for American universities. He thought that the reasons for this phenomenon could be the demands of the universities and standardized tests, but it probably also had more to do with the customs in education. Teachers prepare lesson plans, schools buy classroom sets of certain books, publishers continue to reprint these books, and bibliographies continue to feature them. Therefore, a core of literature is self-perpetuating.

Now that few standardized tests presuppose knowledge of specific titles, there is greater freedom in the teaching of literature. There is evidence of increasing vitality and creativity in the choices used in that teaching of literature. The Young Adult Library Services Association (YALSA), a division of the American Library Association (ALA), has been instrumental in effecting this change by producing lists of new and challenging books that provide alternatives for educators to consider. Librarians, through personal contact with both educators and young adults, recommend and present new titles as well as the tried and true.

Compiling these lists has been a labor of love by dozens of members of YALSA who have willingly, conscientiously, passionately, and thoughtfully prepared them, always with the needs and interests of young adults in mind.

Marjorie Lewis

INTRODUCTION

As the nineties draw to a close and we speed headlong along the information superhighway, there is speculation as to whether books as we know them will survive into the future. Some people argue that our accepted idea of a book is changing. The word *book* today may connote a tape or a disk as well as paper and binding. Nothing that has come along beats the accessibility, convenience, and practicality of the book in the shape with which we are familiar. While the discussion may continue about the physical shape of the book, there is no debate about the way content changes. Those changes, like fashions in dress, food, automobiles, and moral attitudes, keep up with the times. For example, many of yesterday's best-sellers are unknown to today's readers.

To take a retrospective look at lists of books published regularly through the decades is a journey through history. Noting which books last and appear year after year is a sure clue to those enduring characteristics that turn a book from ephemera into what we call "classic"; but one person's classic is another's poison. No one is objective in the choice of classics. All participants in selection of any kind bring their own likes and dislikes to the process. Although they may try their hardest not to let their own feelings enter into their commitment, selectors can't help but indulge in personal feelings and tastes. Reactions to lists are usually predictable. "Where are *my* favorites?" "Why didn't *they* make the list?" "How could they have included that awful book!" All selective lists are personal even though they may have been made by committee consensus. The thing to remember about "best" lists is that they are prepared for your action and reaction. Use a list as a starting place. Take from the list what you need and want. But remember, it is not the last word. *You* have the last word.

Outstanding Books for the College Bound (OBCB) lists are a set of genre-focused lists produced by YALSA since 1959. Although the committees created their own criteria for selection until 1994 (see appendix), OBCB's target audience has always been young adults, ages 12–18, who are planning to continue their education after high school. Librarians report that the bibliographies are also popular with other library patrons—those who have finished college, or who have no plans to go to college, as well as with autodidacts of all ages.

The lists were first produced at the request of the National Education Association (NEA) and were published in the *NEA Journal* in the December 1959 issue. ALA also published them in a brochure format that was sold to libraries to distribute to their young adult patrons, a practice that continues.

Since 1959, thirty-eight editions of the various lists have been produced. In 1984 the existing lists were compiled in a book, *Outstanding Books for the College Bound,* by Mary Ann Paulin and Susan Berlin (ALA 1984). This work supersedes that publication.

The durability and value of the OBCB lists can best be illustrated by an unsolicited testimonial received in the YALSA office not so long ago. A woman called to request the latest edition of *Outstanding Books for the College Bound.* She explained that the lists were not for her, but for her daughter, who wanted to do some background reading to prepare for her college education. When asked how she learned about the lists, she said that she had used them as a teenager and found them so helpful she recommended them to her daughter. *Outstanding Books for the College Bound* is preparing another generation of young adults for higher education.

The criteria for the lists continue to evolve. Over the years, committee members have wrestled with three basic questions: First, what makes a book "outstanding"? Second, who says so? And third, who are the "college bound"?

WHAT IS AN OUTSTANDING BOOK?

An outstanding book contributes to the understanding of civilization as it is in the present, has been in the past, and may be in the future. An outstanding book also presents material in a way that contributes to the appreciation of that which is well done, excellently presented. A book specifically chosen for those planning to continue their education is selected for the list because it is hoped that the book will be part of a foundation of practical, theoretical, or aesthetic experience to be built upon in postsecondary education. Perhaps it presents background material about a current world problem; perhaps it challenges the reader with an electrifying idea; perhaps it engenders a new respect for and interest in another culture; perhaps it encourages a love of beauty and excellence.

The world is not an easy place to understand, to live in, or in which to flourish. The first half of the twentieth century was a period of great change, but the inventions of the telephone, the automobile, and the airplane can't hold a candle to the last half of the century. Such technological advances as a man on the moon, television, space satellites, and microprocessors come to mind. The world today is infinitely smaller; events that occur in the farthest reaches of the earth immediately appear in our own living rooms in full color.

New problems and complex developments require new ways of thinking about people. The continuing debate about what constitutes "family," candid descriptions of all the permutations of sexuality, and the public use of language once forbidden in "polite" society have disturbed traditional values. Crime and poverty have always been with us, but both problems continue to grow to monstrous proportions as we search for solutions. There are no certainties any more. In 1959, one thought one knew when a person was born and when a person died. Not so today. We continue to grapple with decisions about and definitions of life and death. Readers can make better-educated, sensible, sensitive judgments about issues if they have access to a variety of well-written, honest books to help them.

WHO SAYS SO?

Titles for *Outstanding Books for the College Bound* are selected by a committee of members of YALSA. Its members are librarians who serve young adults in various capacities in school and public libraries. Committee members review a variety of selective book lists (e.g., *Best Books for Young Adults*). They read reviews in current newspapers, talk with colleagues and young adults, and remember books that influenced their own lives. The committee members select titles in or out of print published in the English language. They meet at the ALA Midwinter Meeting and Annual Conference over the course of two years. After extensive reading and intensive discussion, they vote to name twenty to forty books they consider the most outstanding in each genre for the final list. Committee members also write the annotations, describing special characteristics and content that will tempt and intrigue young adult readers of the list.

WHO ARE THE COLLEGE BOUND?

"College bound" is open to new interpretation since the inception of OBCB in 1959. The GI Bill, first formulated to benefit World War II veterans, made it possible for returning Korean War veterans to go to college. The United States was trying to catch up with Russia in education after *Sputnik*. Business began to demand college-educated employees. The Civil Rights and women's movements encouraged more people to seek a college education.

These trends were reflected in the growing number of students enrolled in higher education from 1959 to 1994. In 1959, the total enrollment in institutes of higher education was 3,639,847. Of that total, 2,332,617 were male; 1,307,230 were female. In 1994 the total enrollment rose to 14,491,226, of whom 6,526,089 were male and 7,965,137 were female.

It is only since 1976 that numbers reflect the changing ethnicity of college students. White students numbered more than 9 million in 1976 and almost 11 million in 1992. African American enrollment has increased from about 1,033,000 in 1976 to 1,393,500 in 1992. The number of Hispanic students has risen significantly, from 383,800 in 1976 to more than 900,000 in 1992. Figures for Asian or Pacific Island students have also risen dramatically during the same time frame, from 200,000 students to 954,400. Native Americans and Native Alaskans have shown a growth from slightly more than 76,000 in 1976 to 118,000 in 1992.

And the age of college students? We can no longer assume that college-bound students are in their teens and twenties. In 1970, there were 824,000 students over the age of thirty-five registered at higher education institutions; by 1991, the figure had risen to 2,867,000.[1]

In the 1990s, college education has become a right rather than a privilege. Two-year community colleges, evening courses, remedial classes to equip those who have had inadequate high school preparation for college work, programs for adults returning to campuses for career changes or simply for further learning, and college courses on television have made the college experience possible for most people regardless of age, gender, or ethnicity.

The Outstanding Books for the College Bound Committees are continually searching for books that respond to change and innovation and reflect new ways of looking at the world while still remembering the traditional foundations upon which contemporary thought rests.

---

1. All statistics from *Digest of Education Statistics, 1994,* National Center for Education Statistics, U.S. Department of Education, Office of Educational Research and Improvement. NCES 94–115.

USING THE LISTS

These lists are not solely lists of classics, nor are they lists of best-sellers. They will not get a reader into college, but they can make that reader a more educated, concerned, involved person. They are bibliographies of titles that school and public librarians at specific times have selected from hundreds of publications and grouped into a variety of genres that can enrich the reader's understanding of a complex world.

Young adult readers can search among the titles and create a reading list tailored to their interests or, perhaps, find subjects and events with which they'd like to become better acquainted, or people whom they'd like to know better. Annotations are written to catch the readers' interest.

Parents and other interested adults can use these lists to guide their young people's reading as well as their own. Although the lists have been produced for young adult readers, the books are primarily adult titles. These books are not "musts." They are suggestions. By sharing these books with young adults, older adults can form a bridge of discussion and debate between generations, enriching both parties. The year the books appeared on the list is often a clue to the mores, manners, and events of that time. Librarians and teachers can follow literary trends by studying the titles and the lists.

Librarians should not use these lists necessarily as a buying guide, but rather as a guidance tool for readers' advisory service. Teachers will find the lists useful in expanding their curricula. It is recommended that the teachers read the books themselves before assigning or discussing them. It is important to note the time frame in which the book was written, as well as the year in which the book was selected for the list because the understanding of context enriches the reading and enhances both recognition of the author's intent and the reader's recognition of that author's message.

ORGANIZATION OF THE LISTS

The lists are arranged in two ways, by genre and by year of appearance on a list. In Part 1, all of the books selected over the years are combined and arranged by genre. Make no mistake, attaching genre labels to titles can be daunting. The committee for biographies, for example, may have selected a biography of a famous dancer that does not appear under the genre "dance" but rather as "biography." Understanding this, the users can surf the genres, looking at nonfiction annotations or names of people they know to be part of the field in which they are interested. Serendipity is a wonderful outcome of genre surfing.

Within each genre the books are listed alphabetically by title. The dates in parentheses are the original dates of publication or composition. The years of appearance on the lists are also given for each title. Each title is also annotated, the annotations taken from the original lists and written to appeal to young adults. The only bibliographic information given is the title and the author or editor. Many of the titles are available in several editions; some are out of print. For complete bibliographic information and for copies of the books, check your local school, public, or university library.

Part 2 presents the lists themselves, without annotations, beginning with the first lists that appeared in 1959 to the most recent lists, published in 1994. Titles are organized within lists by author or editor name.

The thirty-six books that made the most repeat appearances are featured beginning on p. xiii.

Books tend to appear and reappear, with gaps of years, perhaps, between those reappearances. News stories, films made from books, related books newly published, television adaptations, and historical events affect publication of new editions. Reading the book lists by year can provide signposts to a journey through history.

MOST OFTEN "OUTSTANDING"

The chart below lists books that have appeared with particular frequency on the lists. Some, although written more than a hundred years ago, still have as much to say to today's readers as do current titles. All of them, regardless of the years in which they were written, speak to us in a way that reaches our hearts and minds.

	1959	1961	1963	1965	1966	1967	1968	1971	1976	1982	1988	1991	1994
TEN APPEARANCES													
Austen, Jane / *Pride and Prejudice* (1813)	✓	✓	✓	✓		✓	✓	✓	✓	✓	✓	✓	✓
Fitzgerald, F. Scott / *Great Gatsby* (1925)	✓	✓	✓	✓		✓	✓	✓	✓	✓	✓	✓	✓
Paton, Alan / *Cry, the Beloved Country* (1948)	✓	✓	✓	✓		✓	✓	✓	✓	✓	✓	✓	✓
Twain, Mark / *Adventures of Huckleberry Finn* (1884)	✓	✓	✓	✓		✓	✓	✓	✓	✓	✓	✓	✓
EIGHT APPEARANCES													
Cather, Willa / *My Antonia* (1918)		✓	✓	✓		✓		✓	✓	✓	✓		
Crane, Stephen / *Red Badge of Courage* (1885)	✓	✓	✓	✓		✓		✓	✓	✓			
Curie, Eve / *Madame Curie; a Biography* (1937)		✓	✓	✓			✓	✓	✓		✓	✓	✓
Dostoevsky, Fyodor / *Crime and Punishment* (1866)	✓	✓	✓	✓		✓	✓	✓	✓	✓	✓		
Hart, Moss / *Act One* (1955)		✓	✓	✓	✓	✓	✓	✓		✓		✓	
Keller, Helen Adams / *Story of My Life* (1903)		✓	✓	✓		✓	✓	✓	✓	✓	✓		
SEVEN APPEARANCES													
Frank, Anne / *Anne Frank: The Diary of a Young Girl* (1952)		✓		✓			✓	✓		✓	✓		

(continued)

	1959	1961	1963	1965	1966	1967	1968	1971	1976	1982	1988	1991	1994
SEVEN APPEARANCES (Cont'd)													
Golding, William *Lord of the Flies* (1954)						✓		✓	✓	✓	✓	✓	✓
Hawthorne, Nathaniel *Scarlet Letter* (1850)		✓	✓	✓		✓			✓	✓	✓		
Orwell, George *Animal Farm* (1945)	✓		✓	✓		✓			✓		✓		✓
Salinger, J. D. *Catcher in the Rye* (1951)						✓		✓	✓	✓	✓	✓	✓
Steinbeck, John *Grapes of Wrath* (1939)		✓	✓			✓		✓	✓	✓	✓		
Wilde, Oscar *Importance of Being Earnest* (1895)					✓		✓	✓	✓		✓	✓	✓
SIX APPEARANCES													
Brontë, Emily *Wuthering Heights* (1847)	✓		✓	✓		✓		✓	✓				
Cervantes, Miguel del Saavedra *Don Quixote de la Mancha* (1605)	✓		✓	✓		✓		✓	✓	✓			
Chekhov, Anton *Cherry Orchard* (1904)					✓		✓	✓	✓		✓		
Conrad, Joseph *Lord Jim* (1900)	✓		✓	✓		✓	✓	✓					
Hesse, Hermann *Siddhartha* (1951)								✓	✓	✓	✓	✓	✓
Jenkins, Elizabeth *Elizabeth the Great* (1959)		✓	✓	✓			✓	✓	✓			✓	

	1959	1961	1963	1965	1966	1967	1968	1971	1976	1982	1988	1991	1994
SIX APPEARANCES (Cont'd)													
Kennedy, John Fitzgerald *Profiles in Courage* (1956)		✓		✓			✓	✓	✓			✓	✓
Lee, Harper *To Kill a Mockingbird* (1960)						✓		✓	✓		✓	✓	✓
Maugham, William Somerset *Of Human Bondage* (1915)	✓		✓			✓		✓	✓				
McCullers, Carson *Member of the Wedding* (1946)					✓	✓	✓	✓	✓			✓	✓
Melville, Herman *Moby Dick* (1851)	✓		✓	✓		✓		✓	✓				
Morison, Samuel Eliot *Christopher Columbus, Mariner* (1955)		✓	✓	✓			✓	✓		✓			
Pepys, Samuel *Diary of Samuel Pepys* (1825)		✓	✓	✓			✓	✓	✓				
Sheridan, Richard B. *School for Scandal* (1777)			✓		✓		✓	✓	✓		✓		
Solzhenitsyn, Alexander *One Day in the Life of Ivan Denisovich* (1963)								✓	✓	✓	✓	✓	✓
Stone, Irving *Clarence Darrow for the Defense* (1941)		✓	✓	✓			✓	✓	✓				
Tolkien, J. R. R. *Lord of the Rings* (1965)								✓	✓	✓	✓	✓	✓
Tolstoy, Leo *War and Peace* (1869)	✓		✓			✓			✓	✓		✓	
Williams, Tennessee *Glass Menagerie* (1945)					✓		✓	✓	✓			✓	✓

xv

PART ONE

Outstanding Books by Genre, 1959–1994

The Arts

There are artists (painters, sculptors, photographers), artistes (entertainers or performers), and artisans (makers of things that are decorative or useful). The artist may be an artiste as well, and the artisan can be both an artist and an artisan. Regardless of terminology, they all have an inner drive to create and a need to communicate that experience and its outcome to an audience.

These books are about a wide variety of puppeteers, street performers, clowns, musicians, and dancers as well as the great painters, architects, filmmakers, and photographers of the past and present.

It is their work that brings to our lives fun, beauty, disturbing emotions, and appreciation and regard for another's devotion to artistic endeavor, as well as a singular view of the human condition and unique ways of looking at it.

These books tell about the creators of art and their creations as well as how to appreciate that art. Some describe the preparation and skills that are a part of that wonderful process—making art.

ART, ARCHITECTURE, AND PHOTOGRAPHY

The arts of painting, sculpture, and architecture are arts of space . . . Since space is normally defined as extension in all directions, this attitude can be seen relatively easily in architecture and sculpture, which traditionally are three-dimensional masses . . . The instant a painter draws a line

3

on the canvas, he produces an illusion of the third dimension.

from *History of Modern Art* by H. Horvard Arnason

There is no attempt in the list to cover the development of artistic and architectural form. This is, rather, a compilation of notable books that are of historical and aesthetic interest. Special attention has been paid to art criticism and practical applications. Books on the techniques of photography as well as biographies and examples of photographic works are also found here.

American Art Deco, Alastair Duncan (1986), 1991

This profusely illustrated book explores the tradition of art deco in America.

Annotated Mona Lisa: A Crash Course in Art History from Prehistoric to Post-Modern, Carol Strickland (1992), 1994

From cave paintings to conceptual art, art history is demystified.

Ansel Adams, an Autobiography, Ansel Adams and Mary Street Alinder (1985), 1988

A master of light and images recounts his life and relationships with important photographers of the twentieth century.

Art: A History of Painting, Sculpture, and Architecture, Frederick Hartt (3rd ed., 1989), 1991, 1994

An account of all the artistic endeavors of the Western world reveals the rich heritage left to us.

Art Deco, Victor Arwas (1992), 1994

The style of art deco extends to all the arts—from architecture, painting, and sculpture to crafts and decorations.

Art of Photography, 1839–1989, Mike Weaver (1989), 1991

A catalog of an exhibition looks at 150 years of photography.

Arts of the North American Indian: Native Traditions in Evolution, Edwin L. Wade (ed.) (1986), 1994

A unique and thorough examination details the rich tradition of American Indian art.

Castle, David Macaulay (1977), 1994

Follow the planning and construction of a typical thirteenth-century castle in text and detailed drawings.

Complete Photography Careers Handbook: Expanded to Include Electronic Imaging, George Gilbert (1992), 1994

> Learn about photography as a career.

Exploring Black and White Photography, Arnold Gassan and A. J. Meek (1993), 1994

> The authors instruct the reader on the use of intuition, craft, and analysis in the art of photography.

History of African-American Artists: From 1972 to the Present, Romare Bearden and Harry Henderson (1993), 1994

> A lavishly illustrated volume traces African American artists from the late eighteenth century to the present.

History of Art, H. W. Janson and Anthony F. Janson (1986), 1994

> This story of art is an adventure that enlarges our capacity to understand and appreciate individual painters.

History of Modern Art: Painting, Sculpture, Architecture, Photography, H. Horvard Arnason (1986), 1994

> By tracing contemporary art and architecture through the mid-1980s, Arnason uncovers the varied stories of our modern artistic roots.

How Buildings Work: The Natural Order of Architecture, Edward Allen (1980), 1988, 1991

> A look at the inside of all that brick, concrete, steel—and even straw. A concise, understandable description of how buildings function and behave.

How to Look at Sculpture, David Finn (1989), 1991, 1994

> To understand sculpture, you have to know what to look for.

Images of Nature, Tom Mangelsen (1989), 1991

> Photography captures the glory and wonder of the natural world.

Just Looking: Essays on Art, John Updike (1989), 1991

> Updike gives his personal views of various artists, pieces of art, and diverse artistic items including illustrations of children's books.

Last Traces: The Lost Art of Auschwitz, Joseph P. Czarnecki (1989), 1991

> A Polish photojournalist discovers fine art in drawings, graffiti, and decorations on the walls of various buildings in the Auschwitz concentration camp.

Michelangelo, Howard Hibbard (1975), 1976, 1988

> Michelangelo lives and works in the fourteenth century as a sculptor, painter, architect, and poet.

Modern Classicism, Robert Stern (1988), 1991, 1994

> This description of the modern classical architecture movement uses carefully selected photographs as well as text for better understanding.

More Joy of Photography (1988), 1991

> The 35mm camera user will find the techniques and examples of photographs helpful.

Odyssey: The Art of Photography at National Geographic, Jane Livingston (1988), 1991

> National Geographic pioneers documentary photography and showcases its work in this book.

On the Art of Fixing a Shadow: 150 Years of Photography, Sara Greenough (1989), 1991

> This catalog of an exhibition commemorates photography's sesquicentennial with 450 photographs arranged chronologically and prefaced by essays on photographic periods.

Painting and Sculpture in Europe, 1880–1940, George Heard Hamilton (1978), 1988

> The author surveys modern art in Europe.

Passages in Modern Sculpture, Rosalind E. Krauss (1981), 1988

> Ideas that formed twentieth-century sculpture are examined.

Photographer's Handbook, John Hedgecoe (1992), 1994

> For beginners as well as experienced photographers, this volume explores the full spectrum of photography.

Plain Painters: Making Sense of American Folk Art, John Michael Vlach (1988), 1991

> Folk art and artists influence all aspects of American art.

Power of Photography: How Photographs Changed Our Lives, Vicki Goldberg (1971), 1994

> Photographers and photographs evolve, rather than spring forth fully formed.

Shoot! Everything You Ever Wanted to Know about 35mm Photography, Liz Harvey (ed.) (1993), 1994

> A clear description of 35mm photography develops understanding.

Sweet Flypaper of Life, Roy DeCarava and Langston Hughes (1985), 1988, 1991

> Outstanding photographs and poetic writing combine in a brilliant photo-essay on Harlem in the 1950s.

Why Buildings Stand Up: The Strength of Architecture, Mario George Salvadori (1980), 1988, 1991

> From the pyramids to the skyscrapers, this history of architecture is a readable explanation of why buildings stand up.

Women Artists: An Illustrated History, Nancy G. Heller (1987), 1991, 1994

> This chronicle presents five centuries of painting and sculpture by women, most of whom have been neglected in more traditional art histories.

DANCE

> Drawn from the extraordinary confluence of cultures and peoples that comprise the nation ... American dance has come to reflect the dynamics of a nation where people shape their own destinies through ingenuity and industry, with cross-fertilization and synthesis, individual initiative and renewal, the major sources of its creativity.
>
> from *Dance in America* by Robert Coe

In the four editions of the dance genre bibliographies, there have been a preponderance of books about ballet that include history, the stars, the training, life backstage, and critical comments. Accompanied by glorious photographs, these books respond to the mystique the ballet has always held for young people.

Other books explore modern and postmodern dance as well as tap and jazz dancing. There are also books that portray African American dance at its most dynamic.

101 Stories of the Great Ballets, George Balanchine and Francis Mason (1954), 1982, 1988, 1991, 1994

> An excellent guide to the most famous stage productions, including background for the novice.

Alvin Ailey American Dance Theater, Susan Cook (1978), 1982

> Techniques of ballet, modern, jazz, and ethnic dance are performed by Ailey's company and beautifully portrayed in Cook's black-and-white photography.

American Dances, Agnes de Mille (1980), 1982

> De Mille has drawn a portrait of American classical, ethnic, and popular dance, as performed on Broadway and in film by the great innovators of dance technique.

Ballerina: The Art of Women in Classical Ballet, Mary Clarke and Clement Crisp (1987), 1991

> The role of ballerinas and their great performances enhance the history of the dance.

Ballet and Modern Dance: A Concise History, Jack Anderson (1992), 1994

> A chronicle of Western theatrical dance into the twentieth century includes quotations from dancers and choreographers.

Barefoot to Balanchine: How to Watch Dance, Mary Kerner (1990), 1994

> Understand dance by reading about its history, choreography, and backstage action.

Black Dance in America: A History through Its People, James Haskins (1990), 1991, 1994

> Historical accounts and biographies trace the many forms of African American dance, beginning with its African origins.

Black Dance in the United States: From 1619 to 1970, Lynne Fauley Emery (1980), 1988

> This book chronicles African American contributions to American dance from the arrival of the first Africans to 1970.

Book of Tap: Recovering America's Long Lost Dance, Jerry Ames and Jim Siegelman (1977), 1982, 1988

> A study of tap dancing from its early minstrel and vaudeville days to its golden age in Hollywood, with some thoughts on the future of tap.

Complete Guide to Modern Dance, Don McDonagh (1976), 1982

> A representative anthology of performers and choreographers of the twentieth-century modern dance movement.

Dance Catalog, Nancy Reynolds (ed.) (1979), 1982

> A dancer's compendium that includes listings of dance companies, teachers, colleges, and career suggestions.

Dance in America, Robert Coe (1985), 1988, 1991

> Based on the PBS series, this book traces today's dance back to its roots and then brings the story forward through classical ballet to modern dance.

Dancershoes, Daniel S. Sorine and Stephanie Riva Sorine (1979), 1982

> Dancers stretch, shellac, spray, soak, cut, crush, polish, paint, hammer, and twist their shoes.

Dancing: The Pleasure, Power, and Art of Movement, Gerald Jonas (1992), 1994

Dancing reveals the social, cultural, and religious expression of many cultures.

Danseur: The Male in Ballet, Richard Philip and Mary Whitney (1977), 1982

Spectacular photography enlivens this celebration of the male dancer and choreographer.

Inside Dance: Essays, Murray Louis (1980), 1982

Philosophical, insightful thoughts illuminate the various facets of the dance world—the critics, the travel, and the lifestyle.

Jazz Dance: The Story of American Vernacular Dance, Marshall Stearns and Jean Stearns (1979), 1988, 1991

In writing a history of what seemed to be a dying art, the authors re-awaken an interest in some of the rarely practiced forms of jazz dance, such as the Black Bottom, Lindy Hop, and Buzzard Lope.

Men Dancing: Performers and Performances, Alexander Bland and John Percival (1984), 1988, 1991, 1994

The history of men in dance, highlighting Astaire, Baryshnikov, Cunningham, and many others.

On Your Toes: Beginning Ballet, Wendy Neale (1980), 1982

This book offers practical advice for dancers and their parents and explains the preparations necessary for a dance career.

People Who Dance: Twenty-two Dancers Tell Their Own Stories, John Gruen (1988), 1991, 1994

Interviews give insights into the special world of the dancer.

Private View: Inside Baryshnikov's American Ballet Theatre, John Fraser (1988), 1991

During the 1986–87 season, the ABT has castings, rehearsals, and a national tour.

Prodigal Son: Dancing for Balanchine in a World of Pain and Magic, Edward Villella (1992), 1994

Villella shares his view of ballet as he discloses intimate details of his training, performances, and his relationship with Balanchine.

Push Comes to Shove, Twyla Tharp (1992), 1994

Dancer and choreographer Tharp reveals her dedication to dance, her explorations in movement, and the sources of her creative ideas.

Terpsichore in Sneakers: Post-Modern Dance, Sally Banes (1980), 1982

> Banes looks at the predominant personalities of "post-modern" dance and the techniques that emphasize free movement in an inventive, nontraditional way.

Where She Danced: The Birth of American Art Dance, Elizabeth Kendall (1979), 1994

> The contributions of major innovators and the conditions of their times are the basis for this history of modern American dance.

Winter Season: A Dancer's Journal, Toni Bentley (1982), 1988, 1991

> Ballet can be beautiful to watch, but the dancers suffer to present that beauty.

Worlds Apart: The Autobiography of a Dancer from Brooklyn, Robert Maiorano (1980), 1982

> A dancer bridges the world of his Brooklyn ghetto existence with the glamour of New York's professional dance world.

FILM AND TELEVISION

> Man has always had a compelling urge to make representations of the things he sees in the world around him. As he looks at the creatures that share his daily activities, he first tries to draw or sculpt or mold their forms in recognizable fashion. Then he attempts to capture something of a creature's movements—a look, a leap, a struggle. And, ultimately, he seeks to portray the very spirit of his subject . . . a creation that gives the illusion of life.
>
> from *Art of Walt Disney* by Christopher Finch

The first film and television genre appeared in 1982. Some of the subjects are now outdated. Super 8 moviemaking, for example, has been largely supplanted by the video camcorder. The techniques of film animation have been changed by the computer, but the art by Disney, Hanna-Barbera, John Halas, and Chuck Jones continues to delight. Historical accounts of the rise of Hollywood and its influence on American life are humanized by the biographies and memoirs of film stars.

And So It Goes, Linda Ellerbee (1986), 1988

> Ellerbee details her career in this humorous account of the machinations of the television industry.

Art of Hanna-Barbera: Fifty Years of Creativity, Ted Sennett (1989), 1991

> Cartoon characters including Tom and Jerry, the Flintstones, and Yogi Bear demonstrate Hanna-Barbera's contribution to the development of film animation.

Art of Walt Disney: From Mickey Mouse to the Magic Kingdoms, Christopher Finch (1989), 1991

> Cartoon characters including Mickey Mouse and Donald Duck demonstrate Walt Disney's contribution to the development of film animation.

Chuck Amuck: The Life and Times of an Animated Cartoonist, Chuck Jones (1989), 1994

> Jones's autobiography includes intimate pictures, stills, and text from cartoons.

Citizen Kane Book: Raising Kane, Pauline Kael (1984), 1988

> The shooting script by Herman J. Mankiewicz and Orson Welles explains how the movie came to be.

Cool Fire: How to Make It in Television, Bob Shanks (1976), 1982

> A former producer explains the business and technology of television, the history of the networks, and how programs are planned, produced, and presented.

Elements of Film, Lee R. Bobker (1969), 1982

> An introduction to the technical aspects of filmmaking, including an analysis of the work of sixteen contemporary filmmakers and a discussion of the importance of film criticism.

Film Maker's Guide to Super 8: The "How-to-Do-It" Book for Beginning and Advanced Film Makers, comp. by the editors of Super 8 Filmaker Magazine (1980), 1982

> A collection of articles on equipment, sound techniques and effects, scriptwriting, filming techniques, animation, editing, making documentaries, and more.

Films of Science Fiction and Fantasy, Baird Searles (1988), 1991

> Photographs of movie stills and frame enlargements accompany this description of science fiction and fantasy movies.

Getting into Film, Mel London (1977), 1982

> A career guide covering every aspect of the film industry from production and cinematography to makeup, costumes, and special effects, with information on agents, auditions, education, and unions.

Hollywood History of the World: From One Million Years B.C. to Apocalypse Now, George M. Fraser (1988), 1994

> Hollywood lore enlivens this history, which is illustrated with still photographs.

Hollywood: The Pioneers, Kevin Brownlow (1980), 1982, 1988, 1991, 1994

> A superb history of film and filmmakers from the early days of story-slide shows to the end of the silent picture era, enhanced by unique photographs of actual productions.

Inside Oscar: The Unofficial History of the Academy Award, Mason Wiley and Damien Boda (1986), 1988

> These authors provide an informative and breezy tour through Hollywood, from Oscar's beginning to the 1980s.

Movies, Mr. Griffith and Me, Lillian Gish (1969), 1988

> The colorful, moving memoir of Lillian Gish describes the silent motion picture industry and her innovative director.

Murrow: His Life and Times, Ann M. Sperber (1986), 1988

> The story of the man who set the style and standards for radio and television journalism.

Stunt Man: The Autobiography of Yakima Canutt, Yakima Canutt (1979), 1982

> "Yak" discusses his performance in such films as *Gone with the Wind, Stagecoach,* and *Ben Hur,* giving a fascinating account of the industry, stunting, and special effects.

Technique of Film Animation, John Halas and Roger Manvell (1959), 1982

> This is a complete and illustrated guide to film animation techniques for beginning and advanced filmmakers.

Television, Michael Winship (1988), 1994

> Television pioneers give their special insights into the history of the medium.

They Sang! They Danced! They Romanced!: A Pictorial History of the Movie Musical, John Shipman Springer (1981), 1994

> Illustrations detail the positive and negative aspects of movie musicals.

Toms, Coons, Mulattoes, Mammies and Bucks: An Interpretative History of Blacks in American Films, Donald Bogle (new exp. ed., 1989), 1991, 1994

> African Americans contribute to American films from *Uncle Tom's Cabin* in 1903 to *Do the Right Thing* in the late 1980s.

Video Visions: A Medium Discovers Itself, Jonathan Price (1977), 1982

Video has the potential for educational and artistic use.

When the Shooting Stops . . . the Cutting Begins: A Film Editor's Story, Ralph Rosenblum and Robert Karen (1979), 1982, 1988

The art and profession of editing are described in this autobiographical account of experiences working with filmmakers Woody Allen, Mel Brooks, documentary great Robert Flaherty, and others.

MUSIC

Music is a mystery. It is a potent art . . . it needs intermediaries to make it come to life. By itself, music is merely a series of black notes on a printed page.

from *The Glorious Ones* by Harold Schonberg

The music lists first appeared in 1982. African American music, jazz, Latin American music, country-and-western music, and rock and roll are all represented. Several of the books are about the music business and the nitty-gritty of orchestras and bands. A few teach how to listen to and appreciate all kinds of music. There are, as well, biographies of performers, including instrumentalists, conductors, and singers.

Beatles, Hunter Davies (1968), 1982

An authorized biography of the Beatles, who, as the most influential musicians of the sixties, have left an indelible mark on contemporary music.

Big Band Years, Bruce Crowther and Mike Pinfold (1988), 1991

Jazz greats collaborate to found the big band style of the swing era in the 1930s.

Black Music in America: A History through Its People, James Haskins (1987), 1991

African American music and musicians had an impact historically on other types of music.

Conductors: A New Generation, Philip Hart (1983), 1988

The dreams and realities of orchestra conducting as shown through interviews with the new and rising stars of the profession.

Country Music Book, Michael Mason (ed.) (1985), 1988

More than you ever thought you wanted to know: the history, the stars, the business—the works.

Country Music U.S.A., Bill C. Malone (1985), 1994

> Malone examines country music, including the evolution of country-pop and early country music TV shows.

Demented: The World of the Opera Diva, Ethan Mordden (1984), 1988, 1991

> Temperamental opera stars are praised and denounced by an author with a deliciously wicked point of view.

Glorious Ones: Classical Music's Legendary Performers, Harold C. Schonberg (1985), 1988, 1991

> This book describes and evaluates the legendary performers in classical music, from the castrati to Pavarotti.

Glory Days: Bruce Springsteen in the 1980's, Dave Marsh (1986), 1988

> Continuing observations on the life and career of "the Boss," Bruce Springsteen.

James Brown: The Godfather of Soul, James Brown and Bruce Tucker (1986), 1988

> The "hardest-working man in show business" gives a look at what it takes to be successful when you're born poor and African American in the richest country in the world.

Joy of Music, Leonard Bernstein (1959), 1971, 1994

> Bernstein presents a fresh and enthusiastic approach to the "joy of music."

Latin Tinge: The Impact of Latin American Music on the United States, John Storm Roberts (1979), 1982

> From the tango to disco, Latin American music has influenced American music over the past century.

Making It with Music: Kenny Rogers' Guide to the Music Business, Kenny Rogers and Len Epand (1978), 1982

> This first-rate primer provides an understanding of the components of the music business, with Kenny Rogers adding his personal experiences.

Music and Technology, H. P. Newquist (1989), 1994

> Modern artists chronicle the history and the future of music technology.

Musicians in Tune: Seventy-five Contemporary Musicians Discuss the Creative Process, Jenny Boyd (1992), 1994

> An insider to the music scene interviews the biggest stars.

New Grove Dictionary of Jazz, Barry Kernfeld (ed.) (1988), 1991

> This dictionary provides comprehensive coverage of a distinctly American art form.

Nothing but the Best: The Struggle for Perfection at the Juilliard School, Judith Kogan (1987), 1994

> Revealed are the rigors endured by music students before and during acceptance at the Juilliard School of Music.

Nowhere to Run: The Story of Soul Music, Gerri Hirshey (1984), 1988

> The most recent and definitive look at soul music.

Off the Record: An Oral History of Popular Music, Joo Smith (1080), 1001

> More than two hundred music professionals of the past and present represent all types of music, including jazz, folk, country, pop, and heavy metal.

Orchestra, Michael Hurd (1980), 1982

> The history and development of the orchestra is discussed, and profiles of well-known conductors and coverage of the major orchestras are included.

Pavarotti, My Own Story, Luciano Pavarotti (1981), 1982

> An opera singer rises to superstardom.

Pianist's Progress, Helen Drees Ruttencutter (1979), 1982

> Excellence does not guarantee success at the Juilliard School of Music.

Rock of Ages: The Rolling Stone History of Rock and Roll, Ed Ward, Geoffrey Stokes and Ken Tucker (1986), 1988

> Three rock journalists cover rock and roll from its birth in the 1950s to almost yesterday.

Rock Star Interviews: Conversations with Leading Performers and Songwriters, Petra Zeitz (1993), 1994

> A music journalist presents short biographies and in-depth interviews covering musical careers and the industry.

Rolling Stone Illustrated History of Rock and Roll, Jim Miller (ed.) (1980), 1982, 1991

> *Rolling Stone* magazine presents the history of rock and roll.

Segovia: A Celebration of the Man and His Music, Graham Wade (1984), 1988

> Overcoming prejudice against the guitar as a serious instrument, Segovia becomes the founding father of the modern guitar movement.

Singing in the Spirit: African American Sacred Quartets in New York City, Ray Allen (1991), 1994

> Join Allen at a gospel service as he illustrates the close relationship between gospel and popular music.

Star-Making Machinery: Inside the Business of Rock and Roll, Geoffrey Stokes (1976), 1982

> The accountants and disc jockeys are as important as the musicians in the popular music industry.

Starting Your Own Band, Lani Van Ryzin (1980), 1982

> This no-nonsense guide provides basic information for starting, managing, and promoting your own musical group.

Talking Jazz: An Illustrated Oral History, Ben Sidran (1992), 1994

> Personal memoirs, biographical sketches, interviews, and archival photographs reveal the history of jazz.

Virgin Directory of World Music, Philip Sweeny (1992), 1994

> World music is growing in popularity and is influencing other modern music genres.

Watermelon Wine: The Spirit of Country Music, Frye Gaillard (1978), 1982

> Country music is celebrated, with an emphasis on the performers and their music.

What to Listen For in Music, Aaron Copland (1939), 1982

> The composer provides a basic introduction to the mysteries of musical composition and music appreciation based on a series of lectures.

Willie and Dwike: An American Profile, William Zinsser (1984), 1988

> The stories of jazz musicians, improvisers, and teachers will excite and inspire new musicians.

RELATED ARTS

> It has often been said that the art of puppetry constitutes an international language. I believe it does . . . Ages ago, man learned to differentiate between other creatures' bodily attitudes and facial expressions in order to survive. Opening the eyes in surprise . . . A snarling lip . . . Beefing the brows . . . Sometimes it's a combination of a ridiculous face with a dignified sound that does it, and vice versa. The point is that puppets can go to extremes.
>
> from *Art of the Puppet* by Bil Baird

Puppeteers, street performers, magicians, and clowns are artists who make our lives fun. In the books on this list, dedicated artists talk about their lives and their talents and give tips and secrets for those who'd like to follow in their footsteps. A cheerful stew of entertainment, these books help users appreciate the deceptive simplicity of the true performing artist.

Art of the Puppet, Bil Baird (1965), 1982

A classic description of the art of puppetry as performed by a famed puppeteer.

Big Book of Magic, Patrick Page (1976), 1982

A treasury of tricks for aspiring magicians using cards, coins, rope, paper, rabbits, and . . . presto!

Blackstone Book of Magic and Illusion, Harry Blackstone Jr. (1985), 1988, 1994

The methods and psychology behind every successful trick, including history, techniques, and instructions.

Broadway to Hollywood: Costumes Designed by Irene Sharaff, Irene Sharaff (1976), 1988

Costume designer for Hollywood and Broadway, Sharaff contrasts stage and screen design and compares the fashion and entertainment worlds.

Clowns, John H. Towsen (1976), 1982

A loving look at the clown throughout history and the world, with descriptions of popular clown acts.

Comedy Greats: A Celebration of Comic Genius Past and Present, Barry Took (1989), 1991

The author looks at various geniuses of comedy.

Completely Mad: A History of the Comic Books and Magazine, Maria Reidelbach (1991), 1994

Biographical sketches of contributors dominate this illustrated behind-the-scenes look at *Mad Magazine.*

Making Art Safely: Alternative Methods and Materials in Drawings, Paintings, Printmaking, Graphic Design and Photography, Merle Spandorfer (1993), 1994

Potentially dangerous chemicals and other physical hazards threaten the artist, and Spandorfer reveals alternative materials and methods for safer art.

Mime: A Playbook of Silent Fantasy, Kay Hamblin (1978), 1982

Learn to communicate without words and discover the joy of expressing your ideas with your entire self.

Passing the Hat: Street Performers in America, Patricia J. Campbell (1981), 1982

> Campbell interviews performers whose stage is the street and whose audience is the passerby.

Performance: Live Art 1909 to the Present, RoseLee Goldberg (1979), 1988

> Live art evolves from the turn-of-the-century futurist to punk rock.

Performing Arts: An Illustrated Guide, Michael Billington (ed.) (1980), 1982

> Performing arts include operas, plays, concerts, dance, pantomime, circuses, musicals, magic, puppets, jazz, and much more.

Ringmaster! My Year on the Road with "The Greatest Show on Earth," Kristopher Antekeier and Greg Aunapu (1989), 1991

> A twenty-seven-year-old aspiring song-and-dance man gives a candid account of the year he worked as ringmaster for Ringling Brothers, Barnum, and Bailey Circus.

Staying Power: Performing Artists Talk about Their Lives, Peter Barton (1980), 1982

> Young musicians, actors, and dancers share their experiences, good or bad, in attaining their personal and professional goals.

Treasures of the American Arts and Crafts Movement, 1890–1920, Tod M. Volpe and Beth Cathers (1991), 1991

> Designers, architects, and firms work in ceramics, metals, lighting, and other artifacts of the arts and crafts movement.

THEATER

> I walked toward *Once in a Lifetime* for the last time . . . that final walk every playwright takes toward his play, knowing that it is no longer his, that it belongs to the actors and the audience now, that a part of himself is to be judged by strangers, and that he can only watch it as a stranger himself.
>
> from *Act One* by Moss Hart

Biographies and autobiographies of playwrights and actors offer insight into the theater both as a profession and as an art. And for those interested in the mechanics of theater, there are a number of how-to books written by experts with a love and knowledge of the theater and how it works.

The plays, from *Antigone* to *Zoo Story,* provide examples of the development of drama throughout history. Traditional dramas are well represented as are humorous plays, historical plays, and musicals.

Books about the Theater

Act One, Moss Hart (1955), 1961, 1963, 1965, 1966, 1968, 1971, 1988, 1991

> The author's life up to his first successful play gives the reader many funny and touching moments in the world of the theater.

Actor Prepares, Konstantin Stanislavsky (1936), 1982, 1988, 1991

> Disliking the classical methods of acting, this Russian actor and producer spends his life developing a system in which realism based on the inner truth of a character is essential.

Actors Talk about Acting: Fourteen Interviews with Stars of the Theatre, Lewis Funke (ed.) (1961), 1966, 1968

> Fourteen of America's and Britain's most distinguished actors discuss their profession.

Advice to the Players, Robert Lewis (1980), 1982

> Lewis covers everything from relaxation and energizing to transformation into a complete character.

American Musical Comedy: From Adonis to Dreamgirls, Gerald Bordman (1982), 1988, 1991

> Musical comedy in the United States began in the nineteenth century and continues to evolve as a reflection of musical tastes.

Angry Theater: New British Drama, John Russell Taylor (1962), 1971

> Young dramatists of the 1950s and 1960s discussed here include John Osborne, Anne Jellicoe, Joan Littlewood, Arnold Wesker, David Rudkin, and Harold Pinter.

The Best Plays of . . . , Burns Mantle (annual), 1966, 1968, 1994

> This annual publication gives plot outlines and excerpts from the ten best plays of a given year.

Broadway, Day and Night, Kenneth Marsolais, Rodger McFarlane and Tom Viola (1992), 1994

> Tony Award winners talk about amusing, affecting, and prophetic moments that shaped their careers.

Broadway Musicals, Martin Gottfried (1979), 1982

> An extravaganza of photographs and text demonstrates what makes the show go on.

Caught in the Act, Don Shewey and Susan Schacter (1986), 1988

> Today's finest actors speak candidly about their craft in an inside analysis of the pressure, fame, and struggle for perfection.

Development of the Theater: A Study of Theatrical Art from the Beginnings to Present Day, Allardyce Nicoll (1966), 1971

> Many illustrations accompany this chronological history of the theater.

Fifty Great Scenes for Student Actors, Lewy Olfson (ed.) (1970), 1982

> A collection of scenes for two; ideal for those looking for audition material.

Good Night, Sweet Prince: The Life and Time of John Barrymore, Gene Fowler (1944), 1966, 1968

> John Barrymore is one of America's greatest and most flamboyant actors.

Great Stars of the American Stage: A Pictorial Record, Daniel Blum (1952), 1966, 1968

> This book introduces stage stars with biographies and photos.

Great Theatrical Disasters, Gyles Brandreth (1983), 1988, 1991

> Theatrical calamities include forgotten lines, missed cues, showing up drunk onstage, and collapsing sets falling on leading ladies.

History of the Theatre, Oscar G. Brockett (1991), 1994

> Through both illustrations and text, Brockett provides a comprehensive examination of theatrical heritage.

History of the Theatre, Glynne W. Wickham (1985), 1988, 1991

> The author provides a historical survey of the theater from ancient Oriental, Greek, and Roman times to the twentieth century.

How to Break into the Theatre, Charlotte Harmon (1961), 1966

> The practicalities of becoming an actor, producer, playwright, director, or costume designer are discussed.

I Wanted to Be an Actress, Katherine Cornell (1939), 1966

> A great actress writes about her life in and out of the theater.

Idea of a Theatre: A Study of Ten Plays, the Art of Drama in Changing Perspective, Francis Fergusson (1949), 1971

> Ten plays are analyzed to provide a picture of the art of drama.

James Earl Jones: Voices and Silences, James Earl Jones (1993), 1994

> From a stuttering child to a consummate actor with a world famous, cultivated voice, Jones chronicles his life and theatrical triumphs.

Laurette, Marguerite Courtney (1955), 1966, 1968

> Laurette Taylor wages a successful battle against alcoholism and returns triumphantly to the stage.

Masters of the Drama, John Gassner (1940), 1971

>   Gassner presents the history of drama and describes the people who shaped it.

Musical Theatre: A Celebration, Alan Jay Lerner (1986), 1988

>   An active participant provides a passionate personal history of the musical theater.

Player: A Profile of an Art, Lillian Ross and Helen Ross (1962), 1966, 1968

>   Actors and actresses discuss their lives and careers.

Playwright at Work, John Van Druten (1953), 1966

>   There are practical ways to meet the problems encountered in play writing.

Reflections: Essays on Modern Theater, Martin Esslin (1969), 1971

>   The modern theater is described in a series of essays.

Respect for Acting, Uta Hagen and Haskel Frankel (1973), 1982

>   An actress provides a look at the art of acting and helps an aspiring actor master the techniques of the profession.

Rodgers and Hammerstein Story, Stanley Green (1963), 1966

>   Rodgers and Hammerstein collaborate to produce some of America's best-known musicals.

Same Only Different: Five Generations of a Great Theatre Family, Margaret Webster (1968), 1968

>   The history of English and American theater is seen through five generations of a great theatrical family.

Sondheim, Martin Gottfried (1993), 1994

>   Steven Sondheim, Broadway's musical and lyrical genius, is studied and analyzed through his works.

Stage Crafts, Chris Hoggett (1975), 1982

>   The many detailed illustrations show the student of the theater the techniques of designing and building sets, props, costumes, and much more.

Stage Makeup, Richard Coroson (1989), 1994

>   Makeup artistry is more than assembling the right ingredients, as this illustrated, detailed examination proves.

Theater in Spite of Itself, Walter Kerr (1963), 1971

>   A critic comments on the theater.

Theater of Commitment, Eric Bentley (1967), 1971

Drama is discussed.

Theater of Mixed Means, Richard Kostelanetz (1968), 1971

Kostelanetz examines drama as an art form.

Theater of Revolt: An Approach to the Modern Drama, Robert Brustein (1964), 1971

Brustein discusses the modern approach to drama.

Theater of the Absurd, Martin Esslin (1961), 1971

A new type of drama is examined.

Theatre Backstage from A to Z, Warren Lounsbury (1989), 1994

The author provides an explanation of all that goes on backstage, from props to lights to sets.

Theatre in America: 200 Years of Plays, Players and Productions, Mary C. Henderson (1986), 1988, 1991, 1994

This comprehensive history of American theater begins with showboats and tent shows and ends with Broadway productions.

Theatre: Three Thousand Years of Drama, Acting and Stagecraft, Sheldon Cheney (1959), 1971

The drama of the development of theater unfolds in this historical account.

Theatre World, Daniel Blum (ed.) (annual), 1966, 1968

This is an annual photographic and statistical record of all plays produced on and off Broadway since 1944.

Third Theatre, Robert Brustein (1968), 1968

The dean of the Yale School of Drama discusses off-off Broadway, living theater, and other happenings in the theater.

Towards a Poor Theater, Jerzy Grotowski (1968), 1971

The author presents his methods and training for actors.

Underfoot in Show Business, Helene Hanff (1962), 1982

A witty autobiography describes the funny side of her failures in the world of the theater.

What Is Theater: A Query in Chronicle Form, Eric Bentley (1956), 1971

Bentley attempts to define theater.

William Shakespeare: A Reader's Guide, Alfred Harbage (1963), 1971

Harbage helps the reader understand Shakespeare's works.

Working Actor: A Guide to the Profession, Katinka Matson (1976), 1982

> This guide tells how to choose a school, make the rounds, audition, and choose a manager.

World Theatre in Pictures: From Ancient Times to Modern Broadway, Tom Prideaux (1953), 1966, 1968

> Photographs and essays present a portrait of the theater from ancient times to modern Broadway.

Years Ago, Ruth Gordon (1947), 1966

> Ruth Gordon is stagestruck in Boston.

Young Actor's Workbook, Judith Roberts Seto (ed.) (1979), 1902

> An anthology of scenes and monologues from contemporary plays is provided to use for analyzing a scene.

Musicals

Cabaret, John Kander (1967), 1988

> Decadent prewar Berlin as seen through the eyes of free-living Sally Bowles.

Cats, Andrew Lloyd Webber (1981), 1991, 1994

> Felines from T. S. Eliot's *Old Possum's Book of Practical Cats* portray life from their vantage point on a rubbish heap.

Complete Phantom of the Opera, George Perry (1987), 1994

> This book outlines the history and provides the complete libretto of the blockbuster musical.

Fantasticks, Tom Jones (1960), 1991, 1994

> A teenage couple meet secretly while falsely believing their fathers would disapprove.

Fiddler on the Roof, Joseph Stein (1965), 1968, 1971

> A musical, illustrating the pathos of Jewish life in a Russian village, based on Sholom Aleichem's stories.

Hair, Galt MacDermot (1969), 1971, 1988

> This production was the first tribal rock musical on Broadway.

Hello, Dolly! Jerry Herman and Michael Stewart (1956), 1991, 1994

> This musical based on a Thornton Wilder play follows a marriage broker's attempts to snare another woman's intended husband for herself.

Into the Woods, Stephen Sondheim and James Lapine (1987), 1994

> Cleverly interwoven storybook characters lead a trip of growth and self-discovery.

Jesus Christ, Superstar, Tim Rice and Andrew Lloyd Webber (1970), 1976

> An age-old story is retold in this rock opera version of Christ's impact on the minds of men.

M. Butterfly, David Henry Hwang (1988), 1994

> A brilliant tour-de-force of a twenty-year liaison between a French diplomat and a Chinese opera star—with a startling climax.

Man of La Mancha, Mitch Leigh (1966), 1968

> This musical adaptation of *Don Quixote* centers around a mock trial for the defense of Cervantes while imprisoned and held for inquisition.

Les Miserables, Claude-Michel Schonberg (1987), 1994

> In a musical adaptation of the Victor Hugo novel, tragedy, romance, and poverty trail escaped convict Jean Valjean in the years following the French Revolution.

My Fair Lady, Frederick Lowe (1956), 1966

> Can a girl who sells flowers be transformed into a lady?

Oklahoma!, Richard Rodgers and Oscar Hammerstein (1944), 1966, 1968, 1971, 1988, 1994

> Dance, music, and story are integrated in this look at the settling of the Oklahoma Territory.

Pal Joey, Richard Rodgers (1940), 1988

> This musical tells the story of an ambitious schemer.

Pirates of Penzance, Arthur Sullivan (1879), 1988, 1994

> Must Frederic, a slave of duty, give up Mabel and remain a pirate because of a "most ingenious paradox"?

Quilters, Barbara Damashek (1986), 1994

> Combining music and dance with scenes of dramatic intensity, this play is an eloquent tribute to the courage and spirit of pioneer women.

Sweeney Todd: The Demon Barber of Fleet Street, Stephen Sondheim (1985), 1988

> The demon barber of Fleet Street seeks a grisly revenge.

Threepenny Opera, Kurt Weill (1929), 1988

> Crime pays for Mack the Knife in this musical.

West Side Story, Leonard Bernstein (1957), 1988, 1994

> The Jets and Sharks battle it out in song and dance as Tony and Maria fall in love in this musical based on Shakespeare's *Romeo and Juliet.*

Wisteria Trees, Joshua Logan (1950), 1966

> A member of the Southern aristocracy can't grasp that her way of life is doomed.

Plays

Abe Lincoln in Illinois, Robert E. Sherwood (1939), 1966, 1968

> Sherwood dramatizes Lincoln's life from the time of his romance with Ann Rutledge until he leaves Springfield to become president.

Agamemnon, Aeschylus (c. 458 B.C.), 1991

> After the Trojan War, Agamemnon is murdered by his wife and her lover.

Ah, Wilderness!, Eugene O'Neill (1933), 1966, 1994

> In this comedy a seventeen-year-old faces his first temptations, and his parents try to understand him.

Amen Corner, James Baldwin (1968), 1968, 1991

> Love is a necessity in the African American family, church, and community.

Angel Street: A Victorian Thriller in Three Acts, Patrick Hamilton (1942), 1966

> A scheming husband's nearly successful effort to drive his wife insane and obtain her fortune.

Angels in America: Millennium Approaches (1992); **Perestroika** (1993), Tony Kushner, 1994

> Kushner chronicles AIDS in America during the Reagan era.

Antigone, Jean Anouilh (1944), 1991

> Antigone chooses death because of her fear that compromise will distort and defame life in this contemporary version of the Sophocles tragedy.

Antigone, Sophocles (c. 440 B.C.), 1966, 1968

> A young girl defies the decrees of her uncle, King Creon, and attempts to bury the body of her dead brother.

Arms and the Man, George Bernard Shaw (1894), 1988

> The ugly reality of war intrudes into the life of a romantic young woman.

Arsenic and Old Lace, Joseph Kesselring (1941), 1966

> A comedy about two spinster sisters who quietly do away with old gentlemen who answer their advertisement for boarders.

Barretts of Wimpole Street, Rudolf Besier (1930), 1966

> The romantic courtship and elopement of Elizabeth Barrett and Robert Browning against the wishes of her tyrannical father.

Betrayal, Harold Pinter (1980), 1994

> Beginning in the present and moving gradually backwards, Pinter brings subtlety and insight to the eternal triangle.

Billy Budd, Louis O. Coxe and Robert Chapman (1951), 1966

> Adapted from the Herman Melville story of a young sailor condemned to die by a captain who knows that the young sailor is spiritually guiltless.

Birthday Party, Harold Pinter (1959), 1971, 1976, 1991

> A birthday party destroys a lazy pianist.

Blacks, a Clown Show, Jean Genet (1960), 1976

> African Americans, as caricatures of whites, act out the murder of a white man in a play within a play that hovers between illusion and reality.

Blithe Spirit, Noel Coward (1941), 1988, 1991, 1994

> A rousing comedy that features seances, ghosts, and astral bigamy.

Blood Wedding, Federico Garcia Lorca (1932), 1968, 1971, 1976, 1991

> A Castilian wedding ends in tragedy when the bride runs away with her lover.

Le Bourgeois Gentilhomme, Jean Molière (1670), 1988

> Sudden wealth turns M. Jordan's head and his household into turmoil.

Boys Next Door: A Play in Two Acts, Tom Griffin (1988), 1994

> A social worker supervising four men in a group home finds them touching, funny, poignant, and frustrating, but always human.

Brighton Beach Memoirs, Neil Simon (1982), 1988

> First of an autobiographical trilogy about Eugene Jerome and his family in depression-era Brooklyn.

Buried Child and Seduced and Suicide in B-Flat, Sam Shepard (1979), 1994

> Through a dysfunctional family with a buried secret, Shepard probes deeply into the disintegration of the American dream.

Cavalcade, Noel Coward (1933), 1966

> A pageant of English life from 1899 to 1930.

Cherry Orchard, Anton Chekhov (1904), 1966, 1968, 1971, 1976, 1988, 1991

> The ineffectual Ranevskys exemplify the passing of the Russian aristocracy.

Children of a Lesser God, Mark Medoff (1980), 1988, 1991, 1994

> A young deaf woman falls in love with a hearing man.

Children's Hour, Lillian Hellman (1934), 1988, 1991, 1994

> The sly suggestions of a vicious teenager destroy the tranquility of a girls' boarding school.

Crimes of the Heart, Beth Henley (1982), 1991, 1994

> Three unhappy sisters have strong family ties that see them through their many troubles.

Crucible, Arthur Miller (1953), 1971, 1991

> Teenage girls accused of being witches come to trial in seventeenth-century Salem, Massachusetts.

Cyrano de Bergerac, Edmond Rostand (1897), 1966, 1971, 1988, 1991

> A soldier who is witty and writes poetry is hindered by his own nose.

Death of a Salesman, Arthur Miller (1949), 1966, 1968, 1976

> When a commonplace man who has worshipped the wrong ideals faces his failure as husband, father, and human being, the only solution is suicide.

Deputy, Rolf Hochhuth (1963), 1971, 1976

> Pope Pius XII, Christ's deputy on earth, failed to voice a fundamental Christian principle when he did not publicly condemn Hitler's pogrom, which resulted in the extermination of six million Jews.

Doctor Faustus, Christopher Marlowe (1588), 1966, 1968, 1971, 1976

> In return for pleasure, knowledge, and power beyond the human limit, a learned man sells his soul to the devil and ultimately pays his debt.

Doll's House, Henrik Ibsen (1879), 1976, 1988, 1991, 1994

> Nora, one of feminism's great heroines, steps off her pedestal and enters the real world.

Dream on Monkey Mountain, and Other Plays, Derek Walcott (1970), 1994

> An old man in the West Indies searches for meaning, identity, and relevance.

Effect of Gamma Rays on Man-in-the-Moon Marigolds, a Drama in Two Acts, Paul Zindel (1971), 1976, 1991

> Tillie escapes a nightmarish life by burying herself in a scientific experiment in school.

Elephant Man, Bernard Pomerance (1979), 1991

> Victorian society exploits John Merrick, a grotesquely deformed man.

Enemy of the People, Henrik Ibsen (1882), 1971

> The advanced ideas of a Norwegian town doctor put him in conflict with town authorities and public opinion, causing him to lose his job, home, and friends.

Equus, Peter Shaffer (1975), 1991

> A psychiatrist helps a juvenile delinquent who has blinded six horses and, in the process, finds himself facing complex and disturbing questions.

Everyman, Anonymous (1485), 1971, 1976

> In the best of the medieval morality plays, Everyman is summoned by Death and finds that of all his friends (Fellowship, Knowledge, Beauty, Strength, etc.) only Good Deeds will accompany him.

Father, August Strindberg (1887), 1971

> Sexual conflicts are subtly and thoroughly explored in this naturalistic drama of a destructive marriage.

Fences: A Play, August Wilson (1986), 1994

> A garbageman recalls his career as a Negro League baseball star.

For Colored Girls Who Have Considered Suicide, When the Rainbow Is Enuf, Ntozake Shange (1977), 1994

> The inner feelings of young African American women are captured in this passionate feminist spellbinder.

Foreigner, Larry Shue (1985), 1994

> Nonstop hilarity demonstrates what can happen when a group of devious characters deal with a stranger who supposedly knows no English.

Foxfire, Susan Cooper and Hume Cronyn (1979), 1994

> A 79-year-old Appalachian widow fights to determine her own future as she lives on a mountain farm with the acerbic ghost of her husband.

Front Page, Ben Hecht and Charles MacArthur (1928), 1994

> This comedy of a big city newspaper brings thrills and excitement to reporters and reporting.

Glass Menagerie, Tennessee Williams (1945), 1966, 1968, 1971, 1976, 1991, 1994

> A brother is haunted by the memory of his teenage sister who takes refuge from the world in her collection of glass animal figurines.

Great White Hope: A Play, Howard Sackler (1968), 1971

> Based loosely on the life of African American heavyweight champion Jack Johnson, this prizewinning play serves primarily to illuminate and comment on the prevailing racial attitudes of Johnson's time and today.

Green Pastures, a Fable, Marcus Cook Connelly (1930), 1966

> A fable based on Roark Brandford's novel, *Ol' Man Adam an' His Chillun,* that is a moving African American folk interpretation of the Bible.

Hadrian VII, a Play, Peter Luke (1968), 1971

> An unsuccessful candidate for the Catholic priesthood is later visited by bishops who summon him belatedly to Holy Orders from which point, through a bizarre set of circumstances, he rises meteorically to the eminence of pope.

Hamlet, William Shakespeare (1604), 1966, 1968

> A prince is tormented by uncertainty over whether he should avenge his father's murder.

Harvey, a Comedy in Three Acts, Mary Chase (1955), 1966

> A middle-aged bachelor's friendship with a six-foot imaginary rabbit.

Hasty Heart, a Play in Three Acts, John Patrick (1945), 1966

> A proud and aloof Scottish soldier who does not know that he is dying rebuffs the friendship of five other wounded patients in an army hospital.

Hedda Gabler, Henrik Ibsen (1890), 1966, 1968

> This character study shows a woman of good taste and culture who is spiritually a monster.

Heidi Chronicles, Wendy Wasserstein (1990), 1994

> This hilarious coming-of-age story tells of a successful art historian in a rapidly changing world.

Heiress: A Play, Ruth Goetz and August Goetz (1948), 1966, 1968

> This exciting story tells of a plain girl's conflict with her austere father and a handsome, fortune-hunting suitor.

Hostage, Brendan Behan (1958), 1971

>   A hilarious play about a British soldier who is held hostage in a Dublin brothel in order to prevent the execution of an Irish rebel.

House of Atreus: Adapted from the Oresteia, John Lewin (1966), 1971

>   Each of three classical Greek tragedies by Aeschylus is compressed into one act in this re-creation in modern verse of murder and retribution within a family.

I Remember Mama, John Van Druten (1945), 1966

>   Based on the novel *Mama's Bank Account,* this is a portrayal of a Norwegian immigrant family living in San Francisco at the turn of the century.

I'm Not Rappaport, Herb Gardner (1986), 1994

>   Two octogenarians in New York City are determined not to be "put out to pasture."

Importance of Being Earnest, Oscar Wilde (1895), 1966, 1968, 1971, 1976, 1988, 1991, 1994

>   Can a baby, abandoned in a bag in Victoria Station, grow up to find love, romance, his identity, and the importance of being earnest?

Inherit the Wind, Jerome Lawrence and Robert E. Lee (1955), 1966, 1968, 1971, 1976, 1994

>   The famous Scopes "monkey" trial, argued by a celebrated pair of antagonists, William Jennings Bryan and Clarence Darrow, involves a young teacher in America's Bible Belt charged with blasphemy for teaching Darwin's theory of evolution.

J. B., Archibald MacLeish (1958), 1966, 1968, 1971, 1976, 1991

>   The biblical story of Job is set in a worn, tattered circus, which symbolizes the modern world.

Juno and the Paycock, Sean O'Casey (1954), 1971, 1976

>   The misfortunes of the idle Paycock and his strong wife Juno reflect the Irish dramatist's hatred of war, misery, and death.

King Lear, William Shakespeare (1605), 1991

>   An arrogant old man goes insane after his daughters strip him of every dignity and possession.

Lady's Not for Burning: A Comedy, Christopher Fry (1949), 1976

>   Condemned to burn as a witch, the pretty heroine enchants everybody.

Lark, Jean Anouilh (1953), 1991

> The story of Joan of Arc is retold using flashbacks.

Life with Father, Howard Lindsay and Russel Crouse (1940), 1966, 1968

> Based on Clarence Day's amusing book about his family, especially Father.

Lion in Winter, James Goldman (1966), 1971

> Henry II, his wife, Eleanor of Aquitaine, and their three sons clash in rip-roaring fashion in this interpretation of royal domestic life in twelfth-century Britain.

Little Foxes, Lillian Hellman (1939), 1968, 1971, 1976

> Members of the greedy and treacherous Hubbard family compete with each other for control of the mill that will bring them riches in the post–Civil War South.

Long Day's Journey into Night, Eugene O'Neill (1956), 1968, 1971, 1976, 1988, 1991

> This painfully autobiographical play reveals the illusions and delusions of the Tyrone family.

Look Back in Anger, a Play in Three Acts, John Osborne (1957), 1971, 1976

> Marriage, friendship, rebellion against a stultifying society, and affirmation of life lived lustily are explored by the first of Britain's "angry young men."

Look Homeward, Angel, Ketti Frings (1958), 1966

> An adaptation of the Thomas Wolfe novel about a young man seeking to break away from the stifling world of his youth.

Lost in Yonkers, Neil Simon (1991), 1994

> Two brothers must live with their harsh grandmother when the Great Depression escalates family problems in this bittersweet comedy.

Lower Depths, Maxim Gorky (1902), 1976

> A motley group of derelicts, whose faith in themselves is beyond restoration, huddle together in a basement enduring the misery and despair from which they will never escape.

Lysistrata, Aristophanes (c. 416 B.C.), 1971, 1976, 1988, 1991, 1994

> Is this the ultimate antiwar weapon? Women say "no" to sex in an attempt to end the Athens-Sparta War.

Macbeth, William Shakespeare (1606), 1976

> The consequences of unscrupulous ambition ultimately destroy Macbeth and his lady after they perpetrate an evil crime to gain the Scottish throne.

Madwoman of Chaillot, Jean Giraudoux (1946), 1966, 1968, 1971, 1976, 1991

A madwoman who wants to enjoy the pleasures of daily living devises a plan to save Paris from destruction.

Man for All Seasons, Robert Bolt (1962), 1971, 1976

As a result of his controversy with Henry VIII, Sir Thomas More, a devout Catholic, goes to his death rather than violate his conscience.

Master Harold and the Boys, Athol Fugard (1982), 1991, 1994

Hally, a precocious white South African teenager, lashes out at two older black friends who are substitute figures for his alcoholic father.

Matchmaker, Thornton Wilder (1954), 1991, 1994

A marriage broker attempts to snare another woman's intended husband for herself.

Member of the Wedding, Carson McCullers (1950), 1966, 1968, 1971, 1976

Carson McCuller's famous story about a young Southern girl determined to be the third party on a honeymoon is dramatized.

Midsummer Night's Dream, William Shakespeare (1595), 1971, 1976

Thwarted but determined lovers escape to the enchanted forest where fairies are problem solvers.

Miracle Worker; a Play for Television, William Gibson (1957), 1966, 1968, 1971, 1976

Annie Sullivan's patience and firmness produce a miracle when she frees the brilliant mind of blind and deaf Helen Keller by teaching her to speak.

Misanthrope, Jean Molière (1666), 1976, 1991

The hypocrisy of seventeenth-century Parisian society causes Alceste to become a hermit.

Miser, Jean Molière (1668), 1971, 1994

Satire, humor, and romance combine in a drama of greed versus love.

Miss Julie, August Strindberg (1888), 1976, 1991

Parental, personal, and social pressures force Miss Julie to commit suicide.

Mister Roberts; a Play, Thomas Heggen and Joshua Logan (1948), 1966, 1968

Comic adventures of a crew of a U.S. Navy cargo ship fighting boredom and a stiff-necked captain in World War II.

Moon on a Rainbow Shawl; a Play in Three Acts, Errol John (1958), 1994

Ambition and betrayal lurk in a Trinidad tenement yard.

Mother Courage and Her Children: A Chronicle of the Thirty Years War, Bertolt Brecht (1941), 1968, 1971, 1976, 1991, 1994

> A mother gives up her three children to the Thirty Years' War yet continues to survive because of the war.

Mousetrap, Agatha Christie (1954), 1994

> Stranded in a boarding house during a snowstorm, a group of strangers discovers a murderer in its midst.

Murder in the Cathedral, T. S. Eliot (1935), 1971, 1988

> Friendship, ambition, loyalty, and morality are in conflict in this poetic drama about Henry II and Thomas à Becket.

No Exit, Jean Paul Sartre (1944), 1968, 1971, 1988, 1991

> In this existential drama, we learn that hell is other people.

Noh Drama: Ten Plays from the Japanese Fourteenth and Fifteenth Centuries, Arthur Waley (tr.) (1960), 1988

> A collection of classic Japanese plays.

Odd Couple, Neil Simon (1966), 1971, 1991

> Can two men who are as different as day and night, and who will not change or compromise, live happily together?

Oedipus the King, Sophocles (c. 409 B.C.), 1971, 1976, 1988, 1991

> Here's the original Freudian dilemma. A prophecy is fulfilled when Oedipus kills his father and marries his mother.

Othello, William Shakespeare (1604), 1971

> Jealousy and passion torment a Moorish army commander who loves his wife too much.

Our Town, Thornton Wilder (1938), 1966, 1968, 1971, 1976, 1988

> Love and death in a small town are seen through the eyes of the Stage Manager.

Phaedra, Jean Baptiste Racine (1677), 1971, 1976

> Alceste, the individualist, recognizing the hyprocrisy and emptiness of the social world, seeks a life of solitude in order to protect his integrity.

Piano Lesson, August Wilson (1987), 1994

> An African American family sells an heirloom piano for a plot of land in Mississippi.

Playboy of the Western World, John Millington Synge (1907), 1966, 1968, 1971, 1976

> Believing he has killed his father, a timid Irish peasant boy runs away from home.

Playing for Time: A Screenplay, Arthur Miller (1980), 1994

> A French Jewish singer describes her escape from Auschwitz in this dramatized memoir.

Price, Arthur Miller (1967), 1988

> Two brothers come to grips with the meaning of family, sacrifice, and happiness.

Purlie Victorious: A Commemorative, Ossie Davis (1993), 1994

> To save his people's church, a southern African American preacher must go head-to-head with rich local whites.

Pygmalion, George Bernard Shaw (1913), 1966, 1968, 1988, 1991, 1994

> Professor Higgins bets a friend he can turn common Eliza Doolittle into a duchess.

Raisin in the Sun, Lorraine Hansberry (1959), 1966, 1968, 1971, 1976, 1991

> The sudden appearance of money tears an African American family apart.

Restoration Plays, Robert Gilford Lawrence (1966), 1991

> The Restoration period in England was a great age for drama, especially comedies of manners.

Rhinoceros, Eugene Ionesco (1959), 1971, 1976, 1991, 1994

> The subject is conformity. The treatment is comedy and terror.

Riders to the Sea, John Millington Synge (1903), 1991

> The relentless activity of the sea tragically influences the lives of Irish fisherfolk.

Romeo and Juliet, William Shakespeare (1595), 1988, 1994

> Despite their feuding families, Romeo and Juliet fall in love.

Rosencrantz and Guildenstern Are Dead, Tom Stoppard (1966), 1971, 1991, 1994

> Two bit players from Shakespeare's *Hamlet* are thrust into a terrifying new situation.

Saint Joan, George Bernard Shaw (1923), 1971, 1976, 1991

> A teenage girl shows great innocence in political and religious matters and great genius in military affairs.

School for Scandal, Richard B. Sheridan (1777), 1966, 1968, 1971, 1976, 1988, 1991

> Wit rivals sincerity and hypocrisy rivals true love as Lady Sneerwell, Sir Benjamin Backbite, and Mrs. Candor get their just deserts.

Sheep Well, Lope De Vega (1619), 1991

> The peasant class clashes with the feudal landlords who rule their lives.

Six Characters in Search of an Author, Luigi Pirandello (1921), 1971, 1976, 1988, 1991

> In this avant-garde play within a play, the technique is as important as the plot.

Soldier's Play: A Play, Charles Fuller (1981), 1994

> An African American sergeant's 1944 murder in a Louisiana army camp is investigated by his white captain and a black outsider, with shocking results.

Streetcar Named Desire, Tennessee Williams (1947), 1988

> This is a steamy look at the seamy side of life in New Orleans.

Tempest, William Shakespeare (1611), 1988

> A shipwreck catapults Ferdinand, the duke's son, into romance with the magician's daughter Miranda.

Tooth of Crime: Geography of a Horse Dreamer, Sam Shepard (1972), 1991

> A rising rock musician challenges the reigning star.

Torch Song Trilogy: Three Plays, Harvey Fierstein (1979), 1994

> These plays provide a funny, touching story of a drag queen's desire for a happy, middle-class existence.

Twelfth Night, William Shakespeare (1601), 1988

> In Shakespeare's own words, "If music be the food of love, play on."

Visit, Friedrich Durrenmatt (1956), 1976

> The population's conscience is tested when a rich woman offers her destitute hometown a fortune to murder the man who seduced and betrayed her.

Volpone, Ben Jonson (1606), 1976

> In this satire on greed a rich, childless nobleman pretends to be dying so that those expecting to become his heir will bring gifts.

Waiting for Godot, Samuel Beckett (1952), 1966, 1968, 1971, 1976, 1991

> Two tramps wait eternally for the elusive Godot in this first success of the Theater of the Absurd.

Way of the World, William Congreve (1700), 1971, 1976

> Mirabell and Millamont overcome obstacles on the path toward marriage in this unequaled Restoration comedy that satirizes society and manners.

Winslow Boy, Terence Rattigan (1946), 1966, 1968, 1971

> An ordinary English family takes the problems of its son's expulsion from school all the way to Parliament.

Winterset, Maxwell Anderson (1935), 1966, 1968, 1971

> In depicting the anguish of a young Italian American whose radical father was executed for a murder he did not commit, Anderson is influenced by the Sacco and Vanzetti murder trial.

Woza Afrika: An Anthology of South African Plays, Duma Ndlovu (ed.) (1987), 1988

> These six plays represent the first anthology of recent black South African theater. Each play is built around the political and emotional horror of apartheid.

You Can't Take It with You, George S. Kaufman and Moss Hart (1937), 1966, 1968, 1971, 1988, 1991

> The staid, stuffy parents of Alice's fiancé come to meet her eccentric family on the wrong night.

Zoo Story, Edward Albee (1958), 1971, 1976, 1988

> A terrifying encounter unfolds two strangers who finally "communicate" through violence.

Biography

My mother thinks that a dog I describe as ugly was actually quite handsome. I've allowed some of these points to stand because this is a book of memory, and memory has its own story to tell. But I have done my best to make it tell a truthful story. My first stepfather used to say that what I didn't know would fill a book. Well, here it is.

from *This Boy's Life: A Memoir* by Tobias Wolff

Mark Twain once remarked that there never was a life that was uninteresting and Leon Edel said that good biographies give us an insight into what a person did and the life that made it all possible. What a pleasure it is to meet these people! The tragedy, comedy, and drama of their lives reach across centuries, continents, and generations to us.

This list includes autobiographies, descriptions of lives written by the people who lived them; biographies, accounts of lives written by people who researched and interviewed and pondered the questions of personality and its relationship to action; and collective biographies, short accounts of famous lives grouped around a particular subject.

Abraham Lincoln, Benjamin P. Thomas (1952), 1961, 1963, 1965

The author paints a realistic and sympathetic portrait.

Abraham Lincoln: The Prairie Years and the War Years, Carl Sandburg (1954), 1968, 1971, 1976, 1982, 1988

> Sandburg describes Lincoln's life from his birth in the log cabin on Nolin Creek to his burial at Springfield.

Act One, Moss Hart (1955), 1961, 1963, 1965, 1966, 1968, 1971, 1988, 1991

> The author's life up to his first successful play gives the reader many funny and touching moments in the world of the theater.

All Creatures Great and Small, James Herriot (1972), 1982, 1988

> A rookie veterinarian reconciles the theories learned in school with his "real life" experiences in rural England.

Always the Young Strangers, Carl Sandburg (1953), 1968, 1971

> Sandburg has drawn a sensitive sketch of his early life, especially the problems and thoughts of his teen years.

American Childhood, Annie Dillard (1987), 1991

> A writer tells how her life and writings were influenced by childhood experiences in Pittsburgh during the 1950s.

American Doctor's Odyssey: Adventures in Forty-five Countries, Victor George Heiser (1936), 1961, 1963, 1965, 1968

> The adventures of an American doctor who traveled the world to blot out disease.

American Girl: Scenes from a Small-Town Childhood, Mary Cantwell (1992), 1994

> A successful columnist reminisces about her growing up in a small town in New England.

Anne Frank Remembered: The Story of the Woman Who Helped to Hide the Frank Family, Miep Gies with Alison Leslie Gold (1987), 1991, 1994

> At great risk to their own lives, the Gies family hides the family of Anne Frank in their warehouse attic in Amsterdam, Holland, during World War II.

Anne Frank: The Diary of a Young Girl, Anne Frank (1952), 1961, 1963, 1965, 1968, 1971, 1982, 1988

> The diary of a thirteen-year-old Jewish girl, written in an Amsterdam warehouse attic, where she and her family hid from the Germans during World War II.

Ariel, the Life of Shelley, Andre Maurois (1924), 1961, 1963, 1965, 1968, 1971

> A notable biography of one of England's greatest lyric poets.

At School in the Promised Land; or, The Story of a Little Immigrant, Mary Antin (1916), 1961, 1963, 1965, 1968

A young Russian immigrant relives her experiences during her first days in America.

Atoms in the Family: My Life with Enrico Fermi, Laura Fermi (1954), 1961, 1963, 1965, 1968, 1971

The story of Enrico Fermi, one of the leading physicists in the development of the atomic bomb.

Autobiography, Benjamin Franklin (1791), 1961, 1963, 1965, 1968, 1971

Franklin's witty self-portrait traces his development in work, religion, literature, and public service.

Autobiography, William Allen White (1946), 1961

America in its greatest throes of growth and change is vigorously described by a great journalist.

Autobiography of Alice B. Toklas, Gertrude Stein (1933), 1982, 1988

World War I Paris as seen by Gertrude Stein, the friend of Picasso, Mattisse, Hemingway, and other famous artists of the times.

Autobiography of Benvenuto Cellini, Benvenuto Cellini (1910), 1961, 1963, 1965, 1968, 1971

Italian Renaissance art, sculpture, princes, dukes, and popes are brilliantly presented.

Autobiography of Lincoln Steffens, Lincoln Steffens (1931), 1961, 1963, 1965, 1968, 1971

The associations of a fearless journalist with presidents, kings, city bosses, and dictators.

Autobiography of Malcolm X, Malcolm X (1965), 1976, 1982, 1988, 1994

A revealing, personal account of life in the ghetto, in prison, and as a Black Muslim.

Autobiography of Mark Twain, Mark Twain (1959), 1961, 1963, 1965, 1968, 1971

The life of one of America's most famous humorists.

Baruch, My Own Story, Bernard M. Baruch (1957), 1961, 1963, 1965, 1968

A portrait of an extraordinary man who has never held public office but has been a pillar of strength to four presidents.

Ben-Gurion; a Biography, Robert St. John (1959), 1961, 1963, 1965, 1968, 1971

An absorbing profile of a nation builder who dedicated his life to the service of Israel.

Biko, Donald Woods (1978), 1988

> Woods, editor of the leading antiapartheid newspaper in South Africa, smuggled out the contents of this book about the life, imprisonment, and unsatisfactory inquest into the death of Biko, the charismatic South African leader.

Bismarck: The Man and the Statesman, Alan J. Taylor (1955), 1961, 1963, 1965, 1968, 1971

> A fascinating portrait of a statesman who united the German people by "blood and iron," not by speeches.

Black Boy: A Record of Childhood and Youth, Richard Wright (1945), 1976, 1982, 1988, 1991, 1994

> A moving and harrowing account of growing up in the racist pre–World War II South.

Black Elk Speaks: Being the Life Story of a Holy Man of the Oglala Sioux, John G. Neihardt (1932), 1982, 1988

> A Native American medicine man who survived Custer tells of his visions and the great tribal dances he carried out as a result of these visions.

Blackberry Winter: My Earlier Years, Margaret Mead (1972), 1976, 1982, 1988

> A famous anthropologist relates the events in her life before World War II that affected her as a woman and an anthropologist.

Born on the Fourth of July, Ron Kovic (1976), 1991, 1994

> An all-American boy joins the Marines, goes to Vietnam, is gravely wounded, and becomes an antiwar activist.

Breaking with Moscow, Arkady N. Shevchenko (1985), 1988

> A former Russian spy uncovers layers of Soviet secrets as he describes increasing doubts about his native country and his defection to the United States.

Bridge to the Sun, Gwen Terasaki (1957), 1961, 1963, 1965

> An American married to a Japanese diplomat leads a satisfying life until Pearl Harbor brings tragedy, hardship, and heartbreak.

Bright Eyes: The Story of Susette La Flesche, an Omaha Indian, Dorothy Clarke Wilson (1974), 1976

> A brilliant, educated, and concerned nineteenth-century Indian woman fights against racism, indifference, and atrocities committed by whites.

Bronx Primitive: Portraits in a Childhood, Kate Simon (1982), 1994

> Marked by an unbridgeable generation gap and lack of communication, Simon's difficult Bronx childhood creates great motivation for her writing career.

Cage, Ruth Minsky Sender (1986), 1991

> A teenager comes of age in a Polish ghetto, suffers in a concentration camp, and survives the Holocaust.

Camera Never Blinks: Adventures of a TV Journalist, Dan Rather with Mickey Herskowitz (1977), 1982

> A controversial autobiography by one of the best-known and most respected TV newscasters. Rather's adventures range from his college days in Texas to Vietnam and from his coverage of the Kennedy assassination to *60 Minutes.*

Capote: A Biography, Gerald Clarke (1988), 1994

> Author Truman Capote lived an unorthodox life, as revealed in this candid story.

Charles Dickens, His Tragedy and Triumph, Edgar Johnson (1952), 1982

> Dickens emerges from an impoverished and painful childhood to become an immensely popular novelist and then a social reformer.

Choice of Weapons, Gordon Parks (1966), 1971

> The autobiography of an African American writer-photographer who displays humor, hope, and courage.

Christopher Columbus, Mariner, Samuel Eliot Morison (1955), 1961, 1963, 1965, 1968, 1971, 1982

> Columbus's life and voyages are vividly re-created in this lively narrative.

Clarence Darrow for the Defense, Irving Stone (1941), 1961, 1963, 1965, 1968, 1971, 1976

> This famous lawyer fought not only for mercy and justice but also for social reform.

Coming of Age in Mississippi: An Autobiography, Anne Moody (1968), 1971, 1994

> Living in two-room shacks in rural Mississippi and forced into menial jobs for little pay, Anne Moody learned at an early age the degradation of being African American.

Conspiracy So Immense: The World of Joe McCarthy, David M. Oshinsky (1985), 1988

> Historical background information is given about the "red scare" as well as Wisconsin Senator Joe McCarthy, who personified the anti-Communist movement of the 1950s.

Court Years, 1939–1975: The Autobiography of William O. Douglas, William O. Douglas (1980), 1988

> In this second and final volume, Douglas presents an insider's viewpoint on the workings of the U.S. Supreme Court, describing the interaction between justices and providing information about major decisions.

Dance to the Piper, Agnes de Mille (1952), 1994

> De Mille gives her insider's view as one of America's greatest dance choreographers.

Dark Quartet: The Story of the Brontës, Lynne Reid Banks (1976), 1982

> The brilliant but tortured lives of the three Brontë sisters and their troubled brother is as dramatic as *Jane Eyre* or *Wuthering Heights.*

Darkness over the Valley, Wendelgard Von Staden (1981), 1991

> A teenage German girl aids and befriends concentration camp inmates who work on her family's estate.

Daylight Must Come: The Story of a Courageous Woman Doctor in the Congo, Alan Burgess (1975), 1976

> The moving story of Dr. Helen Rosevear, a doctor and Protestant missionary who strives against tremendous odds and hardships in the Congo from 1950 through 1973.

Days of Grace: A Memoir, Arthur Ashe and Arnold Rampersad (1993), 1994

> A highly respected tennis star and citizen of the world dies of AIDS.

Death Be Not Proud: A Memoir, John Gunther (1949), 1982, 1988

> A father writes lovingly of his bright and promising seventeen-year-old son's long, courageous struggle with a brain tumor.

Diary of Samuel Pepys, Samuel Pepys (1825), 1961, 1963, 1965, 1968, 1971, 1976

> The day-to-day life of a man active in the affairs of London in the 1600s.

Dorothy Thompson: A Legend in Her Time, Marion K. Sanders (1973), 1976

> A fascinating American woman journalist who laughed at Hitler, married Sinclair Lewis, and became a well-known radio commentator.

Double Helix: A Personal Account of the Discovery of the Structure of DNA, James D. Watson and Guntor S. Stent (ed.) (1968), 1971

> The author re-creates the excitement of participating in a momentous discovery and reveals to the nonscientist how the scientific method works.

Dr. Schweitzer of Lambarene, Norman Cousins (1960), 1968

> A well-written description of the doctor's personality, character, and work.

E. B. White: Some Writer!, Beverly Gherman (1992), 1994

> The noted author of *Charlotte's Web,* White is a reserved and witty man who is puzzled by his own success.

Education of Henry Adams, Henry Adams (1907), 1961, 1963, 1965, 1968

> Important events occur and great men are met in Adams's travels in America, England, and France in the latter part of the 1800s.

Einstein: A Centenary Volume, A. P. French (ed.) (1979), 1988

> Essays and letters about Einstein's life, thoughts, and theories help ordinary people understand the genius of this acclaimed nuclear physicist.

Einstein: The Life and Times, Ronald W. Clark (1971), 1976

> The life and career of a great scientist are viewed against the intellectual, political, and scientific background of his age.

Eleanor and Franklin: The Story of Their Relationship, Based on Eleanor Roosevelt's Private Papers, Joseph P. Lash (1971), 1976, 1982, 1988

> A candid and compassionate portrait of a complex relationship that focuses on Eleanor Roosevelt's private role as wife and mother and her public role as First Lady.

Eleanor of Aquitaine and the Four Kings, Amy Ruth Kelly (1950), 1961, 1963, 1965, 1968, 1971

> Political and religious wars and the disastrous Second Crusade are the background of this biography of an extraordinary queen.

Eleanor Roosevelt: First Lady of American Liberalism, Lois Sharf (1987), 1991

> A shy, homely young woman emerges from a privileged, strict Victorian childhood to become an admired and influential woman of the world.

Eleanor Roosevelt: Vol. 1 1884–1932, Blanche Wiesen Cook (1992), 1994

> Born into a privileged world, Eleanor Roosevelt becomes a champion of the underprivileged and a fighter for human rights.

Elizabeth the Great, Elizabeth Jenkins (1959), 1961, 1963, 1965, 1968, 1971, 1976

> A personal history of England's most fascinating queen.

Emma Goldman: An Intimate Life, Alice Wexler (1984), 1988

> A personal and public account of an immigrant anarchist and labor agitator who lived in America in the first half of the twentieth century.

Eric, Doris Lund (1974), 1976

> A mother's poignant account of her teenage son who refuses to give up when he has been struck by leukemia.

Ernest Hemingway: A Life Story, Carlos Baker (1969), 1971

> "The small boy who shouted 'Fraid o' nothing' becomes the man who discovered that there was plenty to fear."

Escalante: The Best Teacher in America, Jay Mathews (1988), 1991

> A dedicated teacher, subject of the movie *Stand and Deliver,* firmly believes anyone can learn calculus.

FDR: A Biography, Ted Morgan (1985), 1988

> In this probing psychological study of FDR's life, the biographer analyzes the forces that shaped an ordinary public servant into a world leader.

Fifth Chinese Daughter, Jade Snow Wong (1950), 1961, 1963, 1965, 1968

> Life in San Francisco's Chinatown and the adjustment a young girl must make between Chinese customs and the modern American way of life.

Florence Nightingale, 1820–1910, Cecil Woodham Smith (1951), 1961, 1965

> After seeing the horrors of the wounded in the Crimean War, Florence Nightingale dedicates her life to worldwide reform of nursing work.

Flush: A Biography, Virginia Woolf (1933), 1968

> An unusual biography of Elizabeth Barrett Browning's cocker spaniel and his interpretation of her life and romance.

Frank Lloyd Wright: An Interpretive Biography, Robert C. Twombly (1973), 1976

> A balanced, integrated examination of Frank Lloyd Wright's life and his contribution to architecture and thought.

Freud: The Man and the Cause, Ronald W. Clark (1980), 1988

> While not definitive, this personal biography offers insight into details of Freud's life that influenced the great thinker's psychoanalytic theories.

Geoffrey Chaucer of England, Marchette Chute (1951), 1971

> A "thrusting, excitable, anxious century" was "blessed by a writer who knew a good joke when he saw one."

George Washington, Man and Monument, Marcus Cunliffe (1958), 1963, 1965, 1968

> Fact and myth are separated in an interpretation of Washington that covers all aspects of his life.

Georgia O'Keeffe, Georgia O'Keeffe (1976), 1982, 1988

> Artist O'Keeffe relates how she dares to live life exactly as she sees it.

Georgia O'Keeffe: A Life, Roxana Robinson (1989), 1991

> A woman artist achieves success and recognition for her work.

Go East, Young Man: The Early Years; the Autobiography of William O. Douglas, William O. Douglas (1974), 1976, 1982, 1988

> The autobiography of a Supreme Court justice who demonstrates his fighting spirit by overcoming poverty and polio to lead the fight for environmental concerns.

Golda: Golda Meir's Romantic Years, Ralph Martin (1988), 1991

> From her early days as a Russian emigrant, Meir journeys through life as an American citizen to become the prime minister of Israel.

Golda: The Life of Israel's Prime Minister, Peggy Mann (1971), 1976

> The amazing story of a woman who was born in Russia, grew up in Milwaukee, went to Palestine at age twenty-three, and ultimately became Israel's prime minister.

Growing Up, Russell Baker (1982), 1991, 1994

> A New York journalist takes a humorous look at his childhood in Baltimore during the depression.

Growing Up Female in America—Ten Lives, Eve Merriam (ed.) (1971), 1976

> A look at the lives of ten women of different socioeconomic backgrounds who were in the forefront of the women's movement.

Hannibal: Challenging Rome's Supremacy, Sir Gavin De Beer (1969), 1971

> This enigmatic military genius plays a crucial role in history.

Hannibal: One Man against Rome, Harold Lamb (1958), 1968

> A comparison of the great Carthaginian leader and the Roman generals who opposed him in his incredible journey across the Alps and his persistent raids in Italy.

Haunted Palace: A Life of Edgar Allan Poe, Frances Winwar (1959), 1968, 1971

> The psychological portrait of the brilliant but controversial poet Edgar Allan Poe.

Having Our Say: The Delany Sisters' First One Hundred Years, Sara Delany and A. Elizabeth Delany with Amy Hill Hearth (1993), 1994

> Two daughters of former slaves tell their stories of fighting racial and gender prejudice during the twentieth century.

Henry David Thoreau, Joseph Wood Krutch (1948), 1961, 1963, 1965, 1968

> The New England yankee sharply criticizes society and becomes one of America's classic writers.

Here I Stand: A Life of Martin Luther, Roland H. Bainton (1950), 1961, 1963, 1965, 1971, 1976

> Martin Luther changes the way the Western world looks at religion.

Hitler, a Study in Tyranny, Alan Louis Bullock (1952), 1976

> This chronicle of Hitler's career includes the rise of Nazism and Germany's role in World War II.

Ho, David Halberstam (1971), 1976

> A short, brilliant portrait of Ho Chi Minh, who twice leads his nation into a successful battle against the West.

Home before Morning, Lynda Van Devanter and Christopher Morgan (1983), 1991

> A nurse serves her time in Vietnam and finds the horror and unpopularity of the war follow her home.

Home to the Wilderness, Sally Carrighar (1973), 1976, 1982

> Hated by her own mother, Sally Carrighar ultimately finds peace and happiness as a naturalist living alone in the wilderness.

Honor Bound: A Gay American Fights for the Right to Serve His Country, Joseph Steffan (1992), 1994

> Steffan, a high-ranking, well-liked cadet at Annapolis, is forced to resign just six weeks before graduation when he reveals he is gay.

I Know Why the Caged Bird Sings, Maya Angelou (1970), 1982, 1988, 1994

> This portrait of the childhood and adolescence of an African American woman is the first in a series of remembrances by actress and poet Angelou.

I, Rigoberta Menchu: An Indian Woman in Guatemala, Rigoberta Menchu (1984), 1994

> Born in Guatemala into abject poverty marked by violence and lack of education, this Nobel Peace Prize winner has become one of the world's foremost fighters for human rights.

In Her Own Right: The Life of Elizabeth Cady Stanton, Elisabeth Griffith (1984), 1988

> The public and private life of a nineteenth-century leader of the women's suffrage movement is portrayed.

Jennie: The Life of Lady Randolph Churchill, Vol. I: The Romantic Years 1854–1895, Ralph G. Martin (1969), 1971

How a girl from Brooklyn, who became the wife of Randolph Churchill and mother of Sir Winston Churchill, exerts extraordinary influence on the rulers of Europe.

John F. Kennedy, Judie Mills (1988), 1991

Overshadowed by his older brother and plagued by ill health, JFK became our youngest president and the symbol of a generation.

John Muir and His Legacy: The American Conservation Movement, Stephen R. Fox (1981), 1988

This study of the "Father of the American Conservation Movement" interprets Muir's life and discusses wildlife preservation.

Kaffir Boy: The True Story of a Black Youth's Coming of Age in Apartheid South Africa, Mark Mathabane (1986), 1991

A teenager comes of age under apartheid in South Africa.

Karl Marx: His Life and Thought, David McClellan (1975), 1976, 1982

The private as well as political life and thoughts of Karl Marx explain much of his great influence on the world.

Ladies of Seneca Falls: The Birth of the Woman's Rights Movement, Miriam Gurko (1974), 1982

Elizabeth Cady Stanton, Susan B. Anthony, Lucy Stone, and others wage a long and stubborn campaign for equal rights.

Lakota Woman, Mary Brave Bird and Richard Erdoes (1990), 1994

Mary Brave Bird stands with two thousand other Native Americans at the site of the Wounded Knee, South Dakota, massacre, demonstrating for Native American rights.

Last Algonquin, Theodore L. Kazimiroff (1982), 1991

Orphaned at thirteen, Joe Two Trees, an Algonquin Indian, chooses to live out his life alone rather than live in the white man's world.

Last Lion: Winston Spencer Churchill, William Manchester (1983), 1988

Beginning with his childhood, this popular biography includes Churchill's experiences during World War I, in Parliament, as Chancellor of the Exchequer, and as a scapegoat of the Gallipoli fiasco.

Let the Trumpet Sound: The Life of Martin Luther King, Jr., Stephen B. Oates (1982), 1988

A biography of the man whose nonviolent protests against racial discrimination began the Civil Rights movement, helping to strike down two centuries of segregation and voter discrimination.

Life and Death in Shanghai, Nien Cheng (1987), 1991

> Nien Cheng tells the story of seven harrowing years in solitary confinement during China's Cultural Revolution.

Life and Death of Mary Wollenstonecraft, Claire Tomalin (1974), 1976

> By not following the rules of eighteenth-century society, Mary was a forerunner of the women's rights movement.

Life of Samuel Johnson, James Boswell (1791), 1961, 1963, 1965, 1968, 1971

> The personality and character of Johnson and the members of his circle.

Lives, Plutarch (c. 120 A.D.), 1961, 1963, 1965, 1968, 1971

> Biographies written around 120 A.D. in which the author parallels the lives of eminent Greeks with those of eminent Romans.

Loss of Eden: A Biography of Charles and Anne Morrow Lindbergh, Joyce Milton (1993), 1994

> The Lindberghs seem to have everything—fame, intelligence, beauty, and money—until tragedy forces them into isolation.

Louis Armstrong: An American Success Story, James Lincoln Collier (1985), 1994

> Born in poverty in New Orleans, Satchmo trains himself to become a great jazz trumpet player.

Madame Curie; a Biography, Eve Curie (1937), 1961, 1963, 1965, 1968, 1971, 1976, 1991, 1994

> The life of an indomitable woman scientist is revealed by her daughter.

Madame Sarah, Cornelia Skinner (1967), 1971

> How a waif from the streets of Paris becomes one of the world's greatest actresses.

Maggie's American Dream: The Life and Times of a Black Family, James P. Comer (1988), 1991

> An African American family achieves the American dream as they move from the segregated rural South to the North.

Malcolm X: The Man and His Times, John Henrik Clarke (1969), 1971

> A good follow-up to his classic autobiography, this collection contains some of Malcolm X's own speeches as well as essays by people who either knew him personally or felt his impact deeply.

Manchild in the Promised Land, Claude Brown (1965), 1971, 1976, 1982

> Brown grows up in Harlem at its ugliest, where street gangs and drugs destroy lives.

Martin Luther King, Jr.: To the Mountaintop, William Roger Witherspoon (1985), 1991

> A great Civil Rights leader struggles to the top of the mountain and sees some of his "dream" realized before he is assassinated.

Mary, Queen of Scots, Antonia Fraser (1969), 1971

> She was queen of Scotland by birth, queen of France by marriage, and almost queen of England.

Mary Shelley: Romance and Reality, Emily W. Sunstein (1989), 1991

> At nineteen, wild, rebellious, and immensely gifted, Mary Shelley creates Frankenstein.

Me Me Me Me Me: Not a Novel, M. E. Kerr (1983), 1994

> This chronicle of the author's adolescent years includes boyfriends, parent problems, and boarding school.

Men of Mathematics, Eric T. Bell (1937), 1961, 1963, 1965, 1968, 1994

> The lives and achievements of world-renowned mathematicians are told with wit and good humor.

Merton: A Biography, Monica Furlong (1980), 1988

> The conflict of his vows as a Trappist monk and what constituted a genuinely religious life is the central theme of this biography.

Michelangelo, Howard Hibbard (1975), 1976, 1988

> Michelangelo lives and works in the fourteenth century as a sculptor, painter, architect, and poet.

Microbe Hunters, Paul Henry De Kruif (1926), 1968, 1971

> Thirteen scientists from Leeuwenhoek to Ehrlich fight disease by discovering and controlling malignant microbes.

Most Dangerous Man in America: Scenes from the Life of Benjamin Franklin, Catherine Drinker Bowen (1974), 1976

> Important moments illuminate the life of Benjamin Franklin.

Mother Jones: The Most Dangerous Woman in America, Linda Atkinson (1978), 1982

> Some call her dangerous, others patriotic, but all would agree that she is unique; a tough union organizer who was still active and outspoken at age ninety.

Mussolini, Denis Mack Smith (1982), 1988

> This study sheds light on the twentieth-century Italian dictator.

My Lord, What a Morning, Marian Anderson (1956), 1961, 1963, 1965, 1968

> This great artist shares her success on the concert stage, her feelings about prejudice, and her hopes for the future of African Americans.

My Place, Sally Morgan (1988), 1991

> Unraveling the mystery of her Australian heritage, Morgan discovers what it means to be an aborigine.

My Several Worlds: A Personal Record, Pearl S. Buck (1954), 1961, 1963, 1965, 1968

> The world-famous author of *The Good Earth* tells how she happened to grow up with both Chinese and American culture.

N. C. Wyeth: The Collected Paintings, Illustrations, and Murals, N. C. Wyeth (1972), 1976

> The life of an American artist is portrayed in words and reproductions of his works.

Nadja, on My Way, Nadja Salerno-Sonnenberg (1989), 1991

> A young classical violinist does it her way.

Naked to Mine Enemies: The Life of Cardinal Wolsey, Charles W. Ferguson (1958), 1961, 1963, 1965, 1968, 1971

> Defying the pope in annulling the king's marriage brings tragedy to Henry VIII's minister.

Napoleon, David Chandler (1974), 1976

> A thorough re-examination reveals much about Napoleon Bonaparte as a man.

Napoleon I, Albert Leon Guerard (1956), 1961, 1963, 1965, 1968, 1971

> No one disputes Napoleon's genius on the battlefield.

Nicholas and Alexandra, Robert K. Massie (1967), 1976, 1994

> A study of Nicholas and Alexandra, last tsar and tsarina of Russia—their reign, their marriage, and their children.

Pablo Picasso: The Man and the Image, Richard B. Lyttle (1989), 1991

> A portrait of Picasso reveals his life as a man and an artist.

Papa Hemingway: A Personal Memoir, A. E. Hotchner (1966), 1976

> Much of Hemingway's personal life is revealed in his conversations with Hotchner.

Part of My Soul Went with Him, Winnie Mandela (1985), 1988

> South Africa's first black woman social worker married Nelson Mandela in 1958 and has carried on his political struggles since his imprisonment in 1962, even though she has been banned by the government.

Paul Revere and the World He Lived In, Esther Forbes (1942), 1961, 1963, 1965, 1968, 1971

> An American patriot lives during colonial and revolutionary times.

Peabody Sisters of Salem, Louise Hall Tharp (1950), 1961, 1963, 1965, 1968, 1971

> The author sketches the Peabody sisters, who did much to develop education in America.

Peron: A Biography, Joseph A. Page (1983), 1988

> The private life and public career of the Argentine dictator who has a well-known wife named Evita.

Peter the Great: Emperor of All Russia, Ian Gray (1960), 1961, 1963, 1965, 1968, 1971

> Peter the Great changes Russia from a medieval to a modern country.

Plain Speaking: An Oral Biography of Harry S. Truman, Merle Miller (1973), 1976, 1982, 1988, 1991

> Always frank, Harry Truman talks about his life, the presidency, history, and other political "fellas" in a biography produced from hundreds of taped interviews.

Portrait of Myself, Margaret Bourke-White (1963), 1976

> A woman newspaper photographer and foreign correspondent valiantly battles Parkinson's disease.

Precocious Autobiography, Yevgeny Yevtushenko (1963), 1968, 1971

> A Russian poet and author describes Soviet Communist society.

Private Demons: The Life of Shirley Jackson, Judy Oppenheimer (1988), 1991

> The author writes about the strange life of Shirley Jackson and her stories.

Profiles in Courage, John Fitzgerald Kennedy (1956), 1961, 1963, 1965, 1968, 1971, 1976

> Profiles of eight U.S. congressmen who risk political oblivion because their moral principles are stronger than their ambitions.

Queen of France: A Biography of Marie Antoinette, Andre Castelot (1957), 1961, 1963, 1965, 1968

> Court intrigue, desperate flight, imprisonment, and death are what Marie Antoinette meets after her marriage to the king of France.

Queen Victoria, Lytton Giles Strachey (1921), 1961, 1963, 1965, 1968, 1971

> The reader meets the queen, the prince consort, and those living during the famous Victorian era.

Quest: The Life of Elizabeth Kubler-Ross, Derek L. T. Gill (1980), 1988

> This Swiss American physician, psychiatrist, pioneer, humanitarian, scientist, lecturer, and mystic is well known as the author of numerous books on death and dying.

R.V.R.: The Life of Rembrandt von Rijn, Hendrik Willem Van Loon (1953), 1961, 1963, 1965, 1968

> A great painter is troubled with tragedy and debts.

Road from Coorain, Jill Ker Conway (1989), 1991, 1994

> Australian outbacker Jill Ker Conway fights for an education and, against the odds, becomes the first woman president of Smith College.

Roosevelt Family of Sagamore Hill, Hermann Hagedorn (1954), 1961, 1963, 1965, 1968, 1971

> Theodore Roosevelt called Sagamore Hill home.

Second Wind: The Memoirs of an Opinionated Man, Bill Russell and Taylor Branch (1979), 1982

> While reflecting on his transformation from an awkward teenager to a college and pro-basketball star, Russell also speaks out on racism, politics, and reading.

Seven Storey Mountain, Thomas Merton (1948), 1961, 1963, 1965, 1968, 1971

> Growing up without a faith, an American poet finds happiness in a Trappist monastery after his conversion to the Church of Rome.

Shakespeare of London, Marchette Chute (1949), 1961, 1963, 1965, 1968

> William Shakespeare is described against the political and cultural background of his age.

Soul to Soul: A Black Russian American Family, Yelena Khanga (1992), 1994

> A young Russian journalist of African American and Jewish heritage analyzes and compares attitudes on race, religion, and sexism in Russia and America.

Sound of Wings: The Biography of Amelia Earhart, Mary S. Lovell (1989), 1991, 1994

> A famous woman flier has two loves—her husband, George Putnam, and flying.

Sound Shadows of the New World, Ved Mehta (1985), 1991, 1994

> Fifteen-year-old Ved Mehta, torn from the world he knows, is thrust into an American school for the blind and manages, despite the differences in cultures, to live the life of a normal teenager.

Story of My Life, Helen Adams Keller (1902), 1961, 1963, 1965, 1968, 1971, 1976, 1982, 1988

> Her sight and hearing destroyed before the age of two, Helen Keller proves that she can still lead a useful life.

Such a Vision of the Street: Mother Teresa—the Spirit and the Work, Eileen Egan (1985), 1988

> Mother Teresa's life—from her childhood in Albania to her world-famous Nobel Prize–winning activities as a hard-working nun with a divine mission to help the poorest of the poor—is shared with a colleague.

Suleiman the Magnificent, Harold Lamb (1951), 1961, 1963, 1965

> Suleiman rules in exotic Turkey in the sixteenth century.

Susan B. Anthony—A Biography of a Singular Feminist, Kathleen L. Barry (1988), 1991

> A woman masterminds the early women's rights movement in America.

They Called Him Stonewall: A Life of Lt. General T. J. Jackson, Burke Davis (1954), 1961, 1963, 1965, 1968

> The life of the Confederate Army's most colorful general is described.

This Boy's Life: A Memoir, Tobias Wolff (1989), 1991, 1994

> A chartered member of the "Bad Boy's Club" tells his story.

This I Remember, Eleanor Roosevelt (1949), 1961, 1963, 1965, 1968

> Eleanor Roosevelt lives in the White House during the crucial thirties and wartime forties.

This Life, Sidney Poitier (1980), 1982

> Academy Award–winning actor Sidney Poitier, the son of West Indian parents, takes chances and breaks rules to finally achieve his dramatic destiny.

This Little Light of Mine: The Life of Fannie Lou Hamer, Kay Mills (1993), 1994

> An African American sharecropper's daughter uses her considerable courage and singing talent to become a leader in the Civil Rights movement.

Thomas Jefferson: An Intimate History, Fawn McKay Brodie (1974), 1976

> The public and private life of one of America's founders is described.

Thomas More: A Biography, Richard Marius (1984), 1988

> This authoritative, popular biography of a Catholic martyr-saint reveals the contradictions in More's character through the author's awareness of modern psychology.

Thread That Runs So True, Jesse Stuart (1949), 1961, 1963, 1965, 1968, 1971

> Jesse Stuart loves teaching.

Three: An Unfinished Woman, Pentimento, Scoundrel Time, Lillian Hellman (1979), 1982, 1988

> Author and playwright Lillian Hellman survives a rebellious childhood in the South, anti-Nazi intrigue, Hollywood romance and glamor, and the effects of blacklisting during the McCarthy era.

Three Who Made a Revolution: A Biographical History, Bertram David Wolfe (1948), 1976, 1982, 1988

> Brief biographies give insight into the lives and thoughts of Lenin, Stalin, and Trotsky, the leaders of the Russian Revolution.

Three Worlds of Albert Schweitzer, Robert Payne (1957), 1961, 1963, 1965

> Albert Schweitzer was a brilliant philosopher, musician, physician, missionary, and writer.

Tisha: The Story of a Young Teacher in the Alaska Wilderness, Anne Pardy (1976), 1982

> Anne Hobbs, a prim and proper nineteen-year-old, arrives in an Alaskan gold-rush town in 1927 to find prejudice, violence, and love.

To Be Young, Gifted and Black, Lorraine Hansberry in Her Own Words, Lorraine Hansberry (1969), 1971

> A writer presents a portrait of herself and her view of the human spirit.

To Dance, Valery Panov and George Feifer (1978), 1982

> Panov, a Russian Jew, defects to the West when, because of his religion, he is not allowed to dance in Russia.

To Destroy You Is No Loss: The Odyssey of a Cambodian Family, Joan D. Criddle and Teeda Butt Mam (1987), 1994

> After the Communists take over Cambodia in 1975, Teeda Butt Mam's upper-class existence is reduced to surviving impossible conditions.

Tolkien: A Biography, Humphrey Carpenter (1977), 1982, 1988

> The life of J. R. R. Tolkien, creator of the mythical world of Middle Earth and its inhabitants, tells of his childhood in South Africa, teaching at Oxford, and fame as the author of *Lord of the Rings.*

True Adventures of John Steinbeck, Writer: A Biography, Jackson J. Benson (1984), 1988

> Benson tells the tale of a Nobel Prize–winning American writer who realistically and romantically captures depression America in print.

Truman, David McCullough (1992), 1994

> Truman's commitment earns America's respect, and this notable president who ends World War II helps reshape a world for postwar peace.

Up from Slavery: An Autobiography, Booker T. Washington (1901), 1961, 1963, 1965, 1968, 1971

> A former slave is determined to build a great school for African Americans in Alabama.

Walls: Resisting the Third Reich—One Woman's Story, Hiltgunt Zassenhaus (1974), 1976

> An anti-Nazi German, Hiltgunt Zassenhaus led three lives in order to aid the Norwegian and Danish prisoners of war during the Hitler years.

What Manner of Man: Biography of Martin Luther King, Jr., Lerone Bennett (1964), 1971

> It was King's achievement to give men hope.

When Heaven and Earth Changed Places: A Vietnamese Woman's Journey from War to Peace, Le Ly Hayslip and Jay Wurts (1989), 1991

> Caught in her country's civil war in a family divided, Hayslip survives imprisonment, rape, starvation, and torture.

Whole World in His Hands: A Pictorial Biography of Paul Robeson, Susan Robeson (1981), 1991

> A granddaughter writes a loving memoir of her brilliant, talented, and controversial grandfather.

William Shakespeare: A Biography, Alfred Leslie Rowse (1971), 1971

> This is an elaborate account of Shakespeare in his age.

Windows for the Crown Prince, Elizabeth Gray Vining (1952), 1961, 1963, 1965, 1968

> The author serves as the first American tutor of the Crown Prince of Japan.

Woman in the Mists: The Story of Dian Fossey and the Mountain Gorillas of Africa, Farley Mowat (1987), 1991, 1994

> Mowat describes the turbulent life and mysterious death of a woman who dedicated her life to the study and survival of endangered mountain gorillas.

Woman Warrior: Memoirs of a Girlhood among Ghosts, Maxine Hong Kingston (1976), 1982, 1988

> The Chinese American experience is passionately portrayed by a young woman who grows up torn between American life in modern San Francisco and the ancient legends, traditions, and folk beliefs of her Chinese heritage.

Woody Guthrie: A Life, Joe Klein (1980), 1982, 1988

> This authentic American folk hero is haunted by family tragedy, misery, and illness.

Wordstruck: A Memoir, Robert MacNeil (1989), 1991

> TV broadcaster MacNeil writes a love letter about the English language.

Yankee from Olympus: Justice Holmes and His Family, Catherine Drinker Bowen (1944), 1961, 1963, 1965, 1968, 1971

> Bowen tells the story of a famous Supreme Court justice and his family.

Yeager: An Autobiography, Chuck Yeager and Leo Janos (1985), 1988

> Mixing boyish enthusiasm with descriptive detail, U.S. Air Force General Chuck Yeager—World War II ace and the first man to break the sound barrier—candidly shares the drama of his life and career.

Zelda: A Biography, Nancy Milford (1970), 1976

> Milford recounts the reckless and painful life of Zelda, from childhood in Montgomery, Alabama, through marriage to F. Scott Fitzgerald, and ending with her many years as a patient in mental institutions.

Fiction

They were careless people, Tom and Daisy—they smashed up things and creatures and then retreated back into their money or their vast carelessness, or whatever it was that kept them together, and let other people clean up the mess they had made.

from *The Great Gatsby* by F. Scott Fitzgerald

There is something in good fiction that lets us see the world as it is, a world that, perhaps, we cannot experience except in our minds. And even though good fiction may go out of fashion, some of it endures through generations.

There are four books that have appeared in all ten editions of the Outstanding Books lists. F. Scott Fitzgerald's book, *The Great Gatsby*, was written in 1925, and the reviews were less than enthusiastic. Fitzgerald's works went "out of style" and often out of print until his rediscovery in the 1950s, some ten years after his death. Jane Austen's *Pride and Prejudice*, written at the beginning of the ninteenth century, still has the power to delight us with its perfect picture of courtship, misunderstandings, and marriages not necessarily made in heaven. Austen's books have been made into movies for the second and third times. *Cry, the Beloved Country*, by Alan Paton, is the tragic story of a black family in apartheid South Africa. We all know *The Adventures of Huckleberry Finn*, whose main character is so much a part of the American scene that some people fail to realize that he was created by Mark Twain and never was "real."

MOST FREQUENTLY SELECTED TITLES

Author	Title
Jane Austen	*Pride and Prejudice* (1813)
F. Scott Fitzgerald	*The Great Gatsby* (1925)
Alan Paton	*Cry, the Beloved Country* (1948)
Mark Twain	*The Adventures of Huckleberry Finn* (1884)

Although the earliest lists include a core of traditional literature accepted as classics by the Western world, there was also recognition of a few best-sellers such as *Gone with the Wind*.

During the sixties the titles selected reflect the vibrancy and excitement of that turbulent decade.

The lists were modernized in the seventies by including such "new" classics as *A Separate Peace* and *Catcher in the Rye*. Even the perennial fantasy favorite, *Lord of the Rings*, was finally included. The addition of newer titles led to hard choices, however; the Brontës were eliminated in the seventies, but reappeared in the eighties.

The eighties continued the trend of fewer core titles and more contemporary titles such as *The Martian Chronicles* and *Going after Cacciato*. In 1988 *The Chocolate War*, which was published especially for young adults, appeared on the list.

Many of the selections in the nineties were books about the lives of people facing physical obstacles as well as a new emphasis on books about and from other cultures. They included *Things Fall Apart* and *Of Such Small Differences*. By 1994 the editions of *Outstanding Fiction for the College Bound* had shaped themselves into a list for all readers needing or wishing to expand their horizons, explain their world (imaginary and otherwise), or enrich their literary pleasure. The 1994 list deleted many traditional titles to make room for the increasing number of books reflecting the dilemmas of the nineties.

In thirty-five years, then, the fiction lists have evolved from a core list of traditional literature to a list containing mainly contemporary literature for young adults who wish to continue their education beyond high school. Readers will find the choices challenging, provocative, and pleasurable.

1984, George Orwell (1948), 1971

In a society of the future, individual privacy is invaded as the "Thought Police" persuade the people that "War is Peace—Freedom is Slavery—Ignorance is Strength."

Accidental Tourist, Anne Tyler (1985), 1991

> Recently divorced Macon Leary, author of a series of guide books for businessmen who hate to travel, chronicles his journey from lonely self-absorption to an accidental new life with a dog trainer from the Meow Bow Animal Hospital.

Adventures of Augie March, Saul Bellow (1953), 1971

> Born out of wedlock, brought up in the poverty of Chicago, Augie takes life as it comes and wherever he can get it.

Adventures of Huckleberry Finn, Mark Twain (1884), 1959, 1963, 1965, 1967, 1971, 1976, 1982, 1988, 1991, 1994

> A Missouri boy tells of adventure on the Mississippi.

Adventures of Sherlock Holmes, Arthur Conan Doyle (1902), 1982, 1988, 1991

> The brilliant, analytical detective Sherlock Holmes and his friend, Dr. Watson, put Scotland Yard to shame as they outwit the villainous Moriarty.

All Quiet on the Western Front, Erich Maria Remarque (1930), 1959, 1963, 1965, 1967, 1971, 1976, 1982, 1988

> Through the eyes and mind of a German private, the reader shares life on the battlefield during World War I.

Ambassadors, Henry James (1902), 1967

> The struggle between the old-fashioned New England conscience and the cultured maturity of Paris is told with subtle irony.

American Tragedy, Theodore Dreiser (1900), 1959, 1963, 1965, 1967

> Ambitious Clyde Griffiths has an affair with Roberta. But Roberta's pregnancy does not fit into Clyde's plan for success, so he drowns her in Lake Michigan.

Animal Dreams: A Novel, Barbara Kingsolver (1990), 1994

> Codi Noline learns secrets about her past that change her future when she returns home to care for her ailing father and to teach high school biology.

Animal Farm, George Orwell (1946), 1959, 1963, 1965, 1967, 1982, 1988, 1994

> A satire on Communism and the totalitarian state.

Anna Karenina, Leo Tolstoy (1875), 1971

> Anna forsakes her husband for dashing Count Vronsky and brief happiness.

Arrowsmith, Sinclair Lewis (1924), 1959, 1963, 1965

> A young doctor must decide between worldly success and money and his own desire to devote his life to scientific research.

Autobiography of Miss Jane Pittman, Ernest J. Gaines (1971), 1988, 1994

> This fictional autobiography tells the story of a remarkable African American woman born in slavery on a Louisiana plantation who is freed after the Civil War and lives another one hundred years to see the second emancipation.

Bear, William Faulkner (1931), 1982

> Ike McCaslin's hunting trips for the legendary bear, Old Ben, are played out against opposing ideas of corruption and innocence.

Beauty, Robin McKinley (1978), 1988, 1994

> An intriguing retelling of a folk story where love is the only key to unlocking the curse and transforming the beast into a man.

Bell for Adano, John Hersey (1944), 1967

> In the Italian village of Adano, Major Joppolo tries to replace the town's bell and gain the respect of the villagers.

Beloved, Toni Morrison (1987), 1991

> Preferring death over slavery for her children, Sethe murders her infant daughter, Beloved, who later mysteriously returns as a young woman and almost destroys her mother's and sister's lives.

Betsey Brown, Ntozake Shange (1985), 1988

> Betsey Brown, full of dreams to change the world, struggles with her loving but conflict-torn family in this enchanting lyrical portrait of three generations of African American women.

Birdy, William Wharton (1978), 1982

> Under the strain of war, Birdy's boyhood obsession with canaries evolves into madness and the conviction that he himself is a bird.

Bleak House, Charles Dickens (1853), 1971

> A woman who is not what she seems, a lawyer who becomes a corpse, and a girl with no past are all part of Dickens's engrossing literary riddle.

Bless Me, Ultima, Rudolfo A. Anaya (1976), 1991

> Ultima, a wise old mystic, helps a young Hispanic boy resolve personal dilemmas caused by the differing backgrounds and aspirations of his parents and society.

Bluest Eye, Toni Morrison (1970), 1994

> Pecola yearns to have beautiful blue eyes like the little white girls she sees.

Bounty Trilogy: Comprising the Three Volumes, Mutiny on the Bounty, Men against the Sea, and Pitcairn's Island, Charles B. Nordhoff and James Norman Hall (1936), 1959, 1963, 1965, 1967

> This great trilogy tells of men who mutiny against an insufferable sea captain.

Brave New World, Aldous Huxley (1932), 1967, 1971, 1976, 1982, 1988

> In this chilling vision of the future, babies are produced in bottles and exist in a mechanized world without soul.

Bride Price, Buchi Emecheta (1976), 1988

> Aku-nna, a very young Ibo girl, and Chike, her teacher, fall in love despite tribal custom forbidding their romance.

Bridge of San Luis Rey, Thornton Wilder (1927), 1959, 1963, 1965, 1967, 1971

> The story of five travelers who are victims of the collapse of a bridge built over a deep chasm in Peru.

Caine Mutiny, Herman Wouk (1954), 1967

> Under the command of tyrannical Captain Queeg, Willie Keith develops from a carefree college boy to a captain distinguished for bravery.

Call of the Wild, Jack London (1903), 1991

> Stolen from his life as a beloved pet, Buck must learn to adapt to abuse as a Klondike sled dog, to life with a loving master, John Thornton, and finally, when Thornton dies, to life in the wild as a leader of the wolf pack.

Catch-22, Joseph Heller (1961), 1976, 1982, 1988

> A broad comedy confronting the humbug and hypocrisy of war and mass society as Captain Yossarian frantically attempts to stay alive despite endless bombing missions.

Catcher in the Rye, J. D. Salinger (1951), 1967, 1971, 1976, 1982, 1988, 1991, 1994

> A ribald, hilarious, and touching tale of a sixteen-year-old's wanderings in New York for three days after he is dropped from his school.

Cat's Cradle, Kurt Vonnegut (1963), 1971

> Finding themselves on the imaginary island of San Lorenzo, a gallery of grotesque people learn about "ice-nine" and espouse a new religion, Bokonism.

Chant of Jimmie Blacksmith, Thomas Keneally (1972), 1991

> Mixed-race Australian Jimmy Blacksmith is brutally betrayed by white society and embarks on a murderous rampage.

China Boy, Gus Lee (1991), 1994

> Kai Ting enters the boxing program at the YMCA and learns how to survive in the tough Tenderloin section of San Francisco.

Chocolate War, Robert Cormier (1974), 1988, 1994

> When Jerry refuses to sell chocolates for a fund-raising drive, he upsets the power structure of his school and becomes the object of a "war" of intimidation and violence.

Chosen, Chaim Potok (1967), 1988, 1991, 1994

> A suspected deliberate bean-ball in a match between two Jewish boys' schools, one Hasidic, the other Orthodox, leads at first to hostility but finally results in friendship and understanding.

Collected Stories of Isaac Bashevis Singer, Isaac Bashevis Singer (1982), 1988

> Short stories that glow with irony, humor, mysticism, and strength, from the renowned Yiddish writer.

Color Purple, Alice Walker (1982), 1994

> In a series of letters to God and her sister, Celie reveals her struggle to overcome the violence and brutality in her life.

Complete Tales and Poems, Edgar Allan Poe (various), 1959, 1963, 1965, 1967

> Outstanding tales of mystery and suspense rise from the pen of one of the great mystery writers of all times.

Count of Monte Cristo, Alexander Dumas (1845), 1959, 1963, 1965

> An adventure story of a man's unjust imprisonment, escape, and return to a new life.

Crime and Punishment, Fyodor Dostoevsky (1866), 1959, 1963, 1965, 1967, 1971, 1976, 1982, 1988

> A sensitive intellectual is driven by poverty to believe himself exempt from moral law.

Cruel Sea, Nicholas Monsarrat (1951), 1959, 1963, 1965

> The story of the courageous crew aboard the *Compass Rose* in the North Atlantic during World War II.

Cry, the Beloved Country, Alan Paton (1948), 1959, 1963, 1965, 1967, 1971, 1976, 1982, 1988, 1991, 1994

> The personal tragedy of a humble Zulu parson seeking his son and sister in Johannesburg.

David Copperfield, Charles Dickens (1850), 1959, 1963, 1965, 1967

> An autobiographical novel reflecting the life of England in the early nineteenth century.

Death in the Family, James Agee (1957), 1971

> The enchanted childhood summer of 1915 suddenly becomes a baffling experience for Rufus Follet when his father dies.

Death in Venice, Thomas Mann (1930), 1976

> A successful author, proud of his work and self-discipline, is forced to confront the mysterious and decadent potential in himself when he becomes infatuated with a frail boy.

Don Quixote de la Mancha, Miguel del Saavedra Cervantes (1605), 1959, 1963, 1965, 1967, 1971, 1976

> The adventures of a mad Spaniard who imagines he lives in the age of heroic knights.

Dracula, Bram Stoker (1897), 1982, 1988

> Count Dracula's nasty practice of drinking the blood of his victim is finally ended by a group of stalwart English.

Dune, Frank Herbert (1965), 1982

> A desert planet is the exotic scene of a richly detailed space fantasy in which the "freemen" of Dune battle the emperor of the known universe.

East of Eden, John Steinbeck (1952), 1991

> The lives of two California families intertwine as good clashes against evil.

Ethan Frome, Edith Wharton (1911), 1959, 1963, 1965, 1967, 1971

> A bitter, stark story of people trapped in a marriage from which they can't escape, though love has long since gone.

Everything That Rises Must Converge, Flannery O' Connor (1965), 1991

> These stories about characters and misfits who live in small southern towns have the effect of an electric shock on the reader.

Fahrenheit 451, Ray Bradbury (1967), 1988, 1991, 1994

> Books are for burning in this future society in which thinking and reading are crimes.

Fall of the House of Usher and Other Tales, Edgar Allan Poe (various), 1976, 1982

> Desolation and impending doom press heavily on these splendid tales of physical horror and psychological terror.

Far from the Madding Crowd, Thomas Hardy (1874), 1982

> Three men seek the love of Bathsheba Everdene in this novel of betrayal and murder in rural England.

Farewell to Arms, Ernest Hemingway (1929), 1982, 1991

> A love story of an English nurse, Catherine Barkley, and Lieutenant Henry, a wounded American ambulance officer, takes place during World War I.

Fathers and Sons, Ivan Turgenev (1862), 1959, 1963, 1965, 1967

> A straightforward novel that dramatizes the conflict and differences between generations in Russia.

Fixer, Bernard Malamud (1966), 1971, 1976, 1982, 1988, 1991

> Victim of a vicious anti-Semitic conspiracy, Yakov Bok is in a Russian prison, with only his indomitable will to sustain him.

Flowers for Algernon, Daniel Keyes (1959), 1971

> After an experiment on a mouse named Algernon triples its intelligence, the same operation is performed on Charlie, a thirty-two-year-old man.

Fools Crow, James Welch (1986), 1988

> Fools Crow, an eighteen-year-old Blackfoot in nineteenth-century Montana, tries to help his people understand the significance of the white "seizers" who threaten the traditional Native American way of life.

For Whom the Bell Tolls, Ernest Hemingway (1940), 1971, 1976

> Robert Jordan, a young American professor fighting for the Loyalist cause in Spain, discovers love, destroys a bridge as assigned, and faces his final test alone.

Forsyte Saga, John Galsworthy (1933), 1959, 1963, 1965, 1967

> The chronicle of three generations of an upper-middle-class English family.

Gathering of Old Men, Ernest J. Gaines (1983), 1991, 1994

> More than a dozen aging African American men claim to be the sole murderer of a southern white farmer and welcome a chance to confound the law after lifetimes of oppression.

Giants in the Earth, Ole E. Rolvaag (1927), 1959, 1963, 1965, 1967, 1971

> The lives of Norwegian settlers in South Dakota.

Go Tell It on the Mountain, James Baldwin (1953), 1976, 1988

> Fourteen-year-old John struggles against the sins of his forefathers and the sensuous evils of Harlem to attain a religious conversion that reflects man's battle for inner peace.

Going after Cacciato: A Novel, Tim O'Brien (1978), 1982, 1988

> Private Cacciato takes off from the Vietnam War to walk to Paris, and his company follows him in a real and surreal journey.

Gone with the Wind, Margaret Mitchell (1936), 1959, 1963, 1965, 1967, 1971

> Scheming, beautiful Scarlett O'Hara and unscrupulous Rhett Butler make this story of the Civil War adventurous and absorbing.

Good Earth, Pearl S. Buck (1947), 1959, 1963, 1965, 1967, 1971

> The trials and problems of a Chinese peasant and his wife.

Grapes of Wrath, John Steinbeck (1939), 1959, 1963, 1965, 1967, 1971, 1976, 1988

> An American farmer and his family leave the dust bowl during the depression to go to California, the promised land.

Great Expectations, Charles Dickens (1860), 1976, 1994

> The hero Pip, reared by humble relatives, is informed he is to be made a gentleman of "great expectations" by a mysterious unknown patron.

Great Gatsby, F. Scott Fitzgerald (1925), 1959, 1963, 1965, 1967, 1971, 1976, 1982, 1988, 1991, 1994

> Lives of wealthy persons in the New York area during the Roaring Twenties are carefully portrayed.

Great Short Works of Joseph Conrad, Joseph Conrad (various), 1976

> Guilt and honor, conscience, and moral justice are explored in these tales of sea adventure and unknown lands.

Green Mansions, W. H. Hudson (1904), 1959, 1963, 1965, 1967

> A romantic fantasy is set in a South American jungle.

Grendel, John Gardner (1971), 1976, 1988

> In a unique interpretation of the Beowulf legend, the monster Grendel relates his struggle to understand the ugliness in himself and mankind in the brutal world of fourteenth-century Denmark.

Gulag Archipelago 1918–1956: An Experiment in Literary Investigation, Alexander Solzhenitsyn (1974–1978), 1976

> Solzhenitsyn examines what life was like for the millions of prisoners in the vast network of penal institutions across Stalin's Russia.

Gulliver's Travels, Jonathan Swift (1726), 1976

> Adventures among the miniature inhabitants of Lilliput, the giants of Brobdingnag, the immortal Struldbrugs, and the reasoning Houyhnhnms form a masterful satire on man and human institutions.

Heart Is a Lonely Hunter, Carson McCullers (1940), 1982, 1988

> The deaf-mute John Singer becomes the talisman for the dreams and yearnings of four people in a small southern town.

How Green Was My Valley, Richard Llewellyn (1941), 1959, 1963, 1965, 1967

> A young Welsh miner watches his idyllic village become a scene of tragedy.

How the Garcia Girls Lost Their Accents, Julia Alvarez (1991), 1994

> The four Garcia girls face a strange new life in America when they are forced to flee the Dominican Republic.

Human Comedy, William Saroyan (1943), 1959, 1963, 1965, 1967

> Saroyan poignantly relates incidents in the life of a family during World War II.

I Never Promised You a Rose Garden, Joanne Greenberg (1964), 1976

> A sixteen-year-old girl struggles out of the seductive kingdom of her madness and reenters the real world.

If Beale Street Could Talk, James Baldwin (1974), 1982

> When Fonny is jailed on a frame-up, he and his girlfriend, Tish, are supported by a loyal family.

In Country, Bobbie Anne Mason (1985), 1991

> Sam Hughes, whose father was killed in the Vietnam War, lives with an uncle she suspects suffers from the effects of Agent Orange. She comes to grips with the impact the war has on her life when she visits the Vietnam War Memorial.

Invisible Man, Ralph Ellison (1952), 1971, 1976, 1982

> A young African American seeking identity during his high school and college days, and later in New York's Harlem, relates his terrifying experiences.

Ivanhoe, Sir Walter Scott (1819), 1959, 1963, 1965, 1967

> The days of Robin Hood and of Saxon and Norman feuds come alive in this story of medieval England.

Jane Eyre, Charlotte Brontë (1847), 1959, 1963, 1965, 1967, 1971, 1982, 1988, 1991, 1994

> An unassuming English orphan becomes a governess and falls in love with her employer.

Joy Luck Club, Amy Tan (1989), 1991, 1994

> A young Chinese American woman realizes her mother's early life in China is an important reason for the rift between them.

Jungle, Upton Sinclair (1905), 1988

> This gritty description of urban life at the turn of the century shows the moral and physical degradation of a "jungle" in which humans barely live better than animals.

Kidnapped, Robert Louis Stevenson (1886), 1959, 1963, 1965

> Scotland after the rising of Prince Charlie is the background for this adventure story.

Killer Angels, Michael Shaara (1974), 1994

> A great battle looms over Gettysburg as the Rebels face the Yanks.

Kim, Rudyard Kipling (1901), 1959, 1963, 1965

> Kipling recounts the adventures of an orphan son of an Irish soldier during days of British rule in India.

King Must Die, Mary Renault (1958), 1991

> The myth of Theseus and the minotaur of Crete comes to life in the form of a novel.

Kristin Lavransdatter, Sigrid Undset (1922), 1959, 1963, 1965, 1967, 1971

> A vivid description of Scandinavian life during the fourteenth century.

Left Hand of Darkness, Ursula K. Le Guin (1969), 1976, 1982, 1988

> First envoy to the technologically primitive world of Winter, Al must deal with a hostile climate; a suspicious, bickering government; and his own conventional sexual mores.

Like Water for Chocolate, Laura Esquivel (1992), 1994

> As the youngest of three daughters in a turn-of-the-century Mexican family, Tita may not marry but must remain at home to care for her mother.

Lincoln: A Novel, Gore Vidal (1984), 1991

> The mosaic of other people's lives in Lincoln's Washington renders a complete picture of the man and his times.

Little Prince, Antoine de Saint-Exupery (1943), 1971

> A strange and mysterious small boy greets a pilot whose plane is forced down in the Sahara and tells him of his own journey to Earth.

Little World of Don Camillo, Giovanni Guareschi (1951), 1959, 1963, 1965

> The half-humorous, half-serious feud between an Italian village priest and a Communist mayor.

Look Homeward Angel; a Story of the Buried Life, Thomas Wolfe (1929), 1967, 1971, 1976

> Hemmed in by the hatreds, jealousies, pretenses, and limited horizons of his family, Gene Gant realizes that he must leave home in order to survive as an individual.

Looking Backward: 2000–1887, Edward Bellamy (1888), 1959, 1963, 1965

> The author's idea of what life will be like in the year 2000.

Loon Feather, Iola Fuller (1940), 1959, 1963, 1965

> Oneta tells of the decline of her Native American world.

Lord Jim, Joseph Conrad (1900), 1959, 1963, 1965, 1967, 1971, 1982

> A man attempts to live with himself after an act of cowardice.

Lord of the Flies, William Golding (1954), 1967, 1971, 1976, 1982, 1988, 1991, 1994

> Innocence ends and savagery begins when English schoolboys are marooned on an ocean island, and they attempt to set up a society of their own.

Lord of the Rings, J. R. R. Tolkien (1965), 1971, 1976, 1982, 1988, 1991, 1994

> Frodo, a young hobbit, descends to the depths of Middle Earth to keep the magic ring from falling into evil hands.

Love Is Eternal, Irving Stone (1954), 1959, 1963, 1965

> The misunderstandings, sorrows, and devotion are revealed in this novel about Abraham Lincoln and Mary Todd.

Lust for Life: The Novel of Vincent Van Gogh, Irving Stone (1934), 1967

> This autobiographical novel reveals the tortured life of Vincent Van Gogh.

Madame Bovary, Gustave Flaubert (1856), 1971, 1991

> Emma Bovary seeks escape from a dull marriage in a novel showing the effect of narrow-mindedness and squalor on a woman's life.

Magic Mountain, Thomas Mann (1927), 1971

> A tuberculosis sanatorium visited by Hans Castorp becomes a symbol of the diseased prewar Europe that made World War I inevitable.

Main Street, Sinclair Lewis (1920), 1967, 1971, 1976

> A young doctor's wife tries to change the ugliness, dullness, and ignorance that prevail in the small town of Gopher Prairie.

Man's Fate, André Malraux (1934), 1971

> A small group of revolutionaries struggles to free the Chinese workers during the conspiracy, bombing, and bloodshed of the Shanghai Insurrection of 1927.

Martian Chronicles, Ray Bradbury (1950), 1982

>   Earthlings gain and lose Mars in these short tales about the colonization of another planet.

Member of the Wedding, Carson McCullers (1946), 1991, 1994

>   A young Southern girl is determined to be the third party on a honeymoon, despite all advice. The novel was published in 1946; the author dramatized it in 1950.

Metamorphosis, Franz Kafka (1916), 1976

>   Gregor Samsa becomes a cockroach.

Mill on the Floss, George Eliot (1860), 1959, 1963, 1965, 1967

>   Impulsive, loving Maggie and her plodding brother, Tom, find in death the solution to their emotional conflicts.

Les Miserables, Victor Hugo (1862), 1959, 1963, 1965, 1967, 1971

>   A powerful story of an unfortunate thief in the underworld of Paris.

Moby Dick, Herman Melville (1851), 1959, 1963, 1965, 1967, 1971, 1976

>   A sea captain vows revenge on the white whale that caused him to lose his leg.

Moonstone, Wilkie Collins (1868), 1959, 1963, 1965, 1971

>   A celebrated jewel is stolen from an idol in a Buddhist temple.

My Antonia, Willa Cather (1918), 1959, 1963, 1965, 1967, 1971, 1976, 1982, 1988

>   A Bohemian immigrant girl faces hardships in pioneer Nebraska.

Native Son, Richard Wright (1940), 1971, 1976, 1988

>   For Bigger Thomas, an African American man accused of a crime in the white man's world, there could be no extenuating circumstances, no explanations—only death.

Nectar in a Sieve, Kamala Markandaya (1954), 1971, 1988

>   Natural disasters, an arranged marriage, and industrialization of her village are the challenges Rukmani must face as the bride of a peasant farmer in southern India.

Northwest Passage, Kenneth Roberts (1937), 1959, 1963, 1965, 1967

>   Major Robert Rogers's tough expedition in 1759 searches for an overland passage to the Pacific.

Nothing but the Truth, Avi (1991), 1994

>   When Philip Malloy hums along with "The Star-Spangled Banner" in homeroom, no one expects a national media event.

Of Human Bondage, William Somerset Maugham (1915), 1959, 1963, 1965, 1967, 1971, 1976

> A young man searches for a way of life.

Of Mice and Men, John Steinbeck (1937), 1982, 1994

> When he accidentally kills a woman, Lennie, a retarded migrant worker, is protected by his friend George.

Of Such Small Differences, Joanne Greenberg (1988), 1991

> Falling in love with an actress propels deaf and blind John into a whole new world of experiences.

Old Man and the Sea, Ernest Hemingway (1952), 1959, 1963, 1965, 1967, 1994

> Santiago, an old Gulf fisherman, battles with a monster marlin.

Once and Future King, T. H. White (1958), 1991

> King Arthur learns his lessons from Merlin the Magician, creates Camelot and the knights of the Round Table, and loves and loses Guinevere.

One Day in the Life of Ivan Denisovich, Alexander Solzhenitsyn (1963), 1971, 1976, 1982, 1988, 1991, 1994

> An inmate lives one day at a time in a Siberian prison camp.

One Flew over the Cuckoo's Nest, Ken Kesey (1962), 1982

> An irrepressible rebel leads fellow inmates of a mental hospital in a struggle with tyrannical Head Nurse Ratched.

Ordinary Love; and Good Will: Two Novellas, Jane Smiley (1989), 1994

> Two modern families in turmoil come to terms with their problems.

Ordinary People, Judith Guest (1976), 1988

> Seventeen-year-old Conrad Jarrett returns home after an attempted suicide and finds his journey back to normal life slow and painful.

Painted Bird, Jerzy N. Kosinski (1965), 1976

> An abandoned dark-haired child wanders alone through isolated villages of Eastern Europe in World War II.

Passage to India, E. M. Forster (1924), 1971

> East and West clash in India when an Englishwoman accuses an Indian man of attacking her.

Pere Goriot, Honoré de Balzac (1835), 1959, 1963, 1965, 1967

> Paris transforms Eugene de Rastignac from a naive provincial to a Parisian gentleman.

Picture Bride, Yoshiko Uchida (1987), 1994

> Taro journeys to America in the early 1900s to marry a man she has never met.

Picture of Dorian Gray, Oscar Wilde (1891), 1967, 1971

> A handsome young man's portrait becomes a mirror, increasingly grotesque, of his true inner self.

Plague, Albert Camus (1948), 1971, 1982

> A small group of people react to the catastrophe of bubonic plague at the Algerian fort of Oran.

Portable Faulkner, William Faulkner (1946), 1991, 1994

> A group of southern families living in an imaginary Mississippi county form a network of relationships with one another.

Portrait of the Artist as a Young Dog, Dylan Thomas (1940), 1988

> A famous poet's youthful escape from the realities of provincial life.

Portrait of the Artist as a Young Man, James Joyce (1916), 1976, 1982, 1991

> A young Irish student struggles to become a writer.

Postman, David Brin (1986), 1988

> Gordon Krantz finds an old, worn postman's uniform after a nuclear holocaust and becomes a symbol of hope to the communities of the American Northwest.

Pride and Prejudice, Jane Austen (1813), 1959, 1963, 1965, 1967, 1971, 1976, 1982, 1988, 1991, 1994

> The romances of the Bennett girls and the ardent desire of their mother to have them all well married.

Prince of Foxes, Samuel Shellabarger (1947), 1959, 1963, 1965

> Italian princes live a life of suspicion and intrigue during the Renaissance.

Queen's Gambit, Walter S. Tevis (1983), 1991

> Beth Harmon is taught to play chess by the janitor in her orphanage. She jeopardizes her achievements by personal doubts and dependence on drugs and alcohol.

Quo Vadis, Henryk Sienkiewicz (1896), 1959, 1963, 1965, 1967

> The immorality of the first-century Romans is a contrast to the purity of the Christians in ancient Rome.

Ragtime, E. L. Doctorow (1975), 1991

> Real and fictional people from widely different economic and ethnic groups interact in nineteenth-century America.

Rebecca, Daphne Du Maurier (1938), 1982

> The timid new mistress of Manderley is haunted by the shadow of her predecessor, the vibrant Rebecca.

Red Badge of Courage, Stephen Crane (1885), 1959, 1963, 1965, 1967, 1971, 1976, 1982, 1988

> A boy moves from cowardice to courage in the Civil War.

Reivers: A Reminiscence, William Faulkner (1962), 1988

> In 1905, eleven-year-old Lucius and two other "reivers," or plunderers, steal his grandfather's car and set off for Memphis and misadventure.

Return of the Native, Thomas Hardy (1878), 1959, 1963, 1965, 1967, 1976

> The powerful influence of Egdon Heath turns to tragedy the love of Clym and Eustacia and brings ruin to others as well.

Scarlet Letter, Nathaniel Hawthorne (1850), 1959, 1963, 1965, 1967, 1976, 1982, 1988

> Hester Prynne and her lover feel the effects of sin in Puritan New England.

Schindler's List, Thomas Keneally (1982), 1988

> Oskar Schindler, a rich factory owner, risks his life and spends his personal fortune to save Jews listed as his workers during World War II.

Sea of Grass, Conrad Richter (1936), 1959, 1963, 1965, 1967

> Cattlemen and homesteaders fight for land and grazing rights.

Selected Tales, Edgar Allan Poe (1980), 1994

> These chilling tales of the supernatural are not for the nervous.

Separate Peace, John Knowles (1959), 1967, 1971, 1976, 1982

> Against the backdrop of World War II, the rivalry of two roommates at a boys' school turns into a private war.

Siddhartha, Hermann Hesse (1951), 1976, 1982, 1988, 1991, 1994

> Emerging from a kaleidoscope of experiences and tasted pleasures, Siddhartha transcends to a state of peace and mystic holiness in this strangely simple story.

Single Pebble, John Hersey (1956), 1959, 1963, 1965

> An American engineer finds Oriental philosophy a greater obstacle than the wild Yangtze River.

Slaughterhouse Five; or, The Children's Crusade, Kurt Vonnegut (1969), 1976, 1982, 1988, 1994

> Billy Pilgrim, an optometrist from Ilium, New York, shuttles between the cellars of Dresden, smoldering from Allied bombardment, and a luxurious zoo on the planet Tralfamadore.

Slave, Isaac Bashevis Singer (1962), 1982

> Forbidden love and suffering teach Jacob wisdom and strength.

Sons and Lovers, David Herbert Lawrence (1913), 1971, 1976

> Neither of Paul Morel's two lovers can wean him away from the stifling influence of excessive mother-love.

Sound and the Fury, William Faulkner (1929), 1907, 1971, 1970

> The tragic life of the Compsons, a degenerate Southern family, is described by Benjy, a thirty-three-year-old idiot.

Sound of Waves, Yukio Mishima (1956), 1971, 1988

> This work delicately traces the lives of two young lovers on a small, traditional Japanese island untouched by modern civilization.

Spring Moon: A Novel of China, Bette B. Lord (1981), 1988

> Spring Moon's pampered, easy life changes as China changes.

Steppenwolf, Hermann Hesse (1921), 1971

> Considering himself half-man, half-wolf of the steppes, Harry Haller faces the conflict between nature and spirit.

Storm, George Stewart (1947), 1959, 1963, 1965

> A hurricane forms at sea.

Strange Case of Dr. Jekyll and Mr. Hyde, Robert Louis Stevenson (1886), 1967

> Dr. Jekyll discovers a drug that will create a separate personality that will absorb all of his evil characteristics. He calls him Mr. Hyde.

Stranger, Albert Camus (1946), 1967, 1976, 1991, 1994

> An ordinary little clerk lives quietly, unemotionally, until he becomes involved in another man's passions, commits an absurd murder, and is sentenced to death.

Tale of Two Cities, Charles Dickens (1859), 1982, 1988

> The lives of Alexander Manette and his daughter Lucie and those of Charles Darnay and Sydney Carton become entangled during the French Revolution.

Tales of Terror: Ten Short Stories, Edgar Allan Poe (1985), 1988

> Ten of Poe's terrifying tales are told in this collection.

Tell Me a Riddle, Tillie Olsen (1960), 1982

> Four unpretentious stories feature the very young, the mature, the dying, and the poor.

Things Fall Apart, Chinua Achebe (1959), 1991, 1994

> European missionaries and colonial officials disrupt the patterns and rituals of traditional Nigerian Ibo society at the end of the nineteenth century.

Things Invisible to See, Nancy Willard (1985), 1988

> In Paradise, on the banks of the River of Time, the Lord of the Universe is playing ball with his archangels; and in Ann Arbor, Michigan, Ben Harkissan is hitting a baseball that strikes Clare Bishop, paralyzing her—an act that entwines the characters in "things invisible."

Time and Again, Jack Finney (1970), 1982, 1988

> Simon Morley travels back in time to New York of the 1880s.

Tin Drum, Günter Grass (1961), 1971

> Oskar, who stops growing when he is three, describes life in Germany during and after World War II.

To Kill a Mockingbird, Harper Lee (1960), 1967, 1971, 1982, 1988, 1991, 1994

> A young girl tells of life in a small Alabama town and her father's defense in court of an African American accused of raping a white woman.

Tree of Liberty, Elizabeth Page (1939), 1959, 1963, 1965, 1967

> Page provides a saga of an American family from the days of the colonies to the western plains.

Trial, Franz Kafka (1925), 1971

> Joseph K., a bank official, is arrested, tried, and convicted of an unnamed crime of which he knows nothing.

Turn of the Screw, Henry James (1891), 1971

> A governess tries to break the spell she believes evil spirits have cast over the two innocent children in her care.

Vanity Fair: A Novel without a Hero, William Makepeace Thackeray (1847), 1959, 1963, 1965, 1967

> Becky Sharp is an ambitious social climber in Victorian London.

Vein of Iron, Ellen Glasgow (1935), 1959, 1963, 1965

> A family "vein of iron" runs in Ada, indomitable daughter of a Virginia family.

Wall, John Hersey (1950), 1982

> The doomed Jews of the Warsaw ghetto turn and face their oppressors.

War and Peace, Leo Tolstoy (1869), 1959, 1963, 1965, 1967, 1976, 1982

> When Napoleon invades Russia, characters both real and fictional find their lives changed.

Way of All Flesh, Samuel Butler (1903), 1959, 1963, 1965, 1967

> The son of a strict clergyman breaks parental ties, thereby freeing himself to make his own way of life.

Way past Cool: A Novel, Jess Mowry (1992), 1994

> Thirteen-year-old Gordon is the leader of a gang of African American boys struggling to hold a few blocks of bleak turf in Oakland, California.

When the Legends Die, Hal Borland (1963), 1982

> Embittered by the white man's deceits, Thomas Black Bull punishes the rodeo horses he rides until he has a crushing accident.

Wuthering Heights, Emily Brontë (1847), 1959, 1963, 1965, 1967, 1971, 1982

> A story of intense and frustrated love, of hate and revenge, that takes place in the wild moors of England.

Yearling, Marjorie Kinnan Rawlings (1938), 1959, 1963, 1965

> Life is hard for crippled Jody, who lives in the Florida backcountry.

Yellow Raft on Blue Water, Michael Dorris (1987), 1991, 1994

> At times separated by hardships and angry secrets but always bonded by kinship, three generations of Native American women tell their stories in their search for self-identity.

Zorba the Greek, Nikos Kazantzakis (1952), 1971

> As manager of a mine in Crete, Zorba—philosopher and roué—accomplishes fantastic feats of physical prowess, tells wild stories of his erotic adventures, misbehaves badly with the owner's money, sings, dances, and talks of the world.

Nonfiction

I think it's really important that young people today understand that the movement of the sixties was really a people's
movement. The media and history seem to record it as Martin Luther King's movement, but young people should realize that it was people just like them, their age, that formulated goals and strategies, and actually developed the
movement. When they look around now, and see things that
need to be changed, they should say: "What can I do?"

from an interview with Diane Nash
in *Eyes on the Prize*

The standard caveat among librarians weeding a collection (de-
ciding which books to discard) is, "If you find a book that says
'Someday man will go to the moon,' think twice about keeping
it." The same warning holds true for a reader. In using retrospective
bibliographies of nonfiction, the reader must keep in mind *when* the
book was written.

The first nonfiction *Outstanding Books for the College Bound* list
was published in 1971. That first list included many books that en-
compassed a wide variety of topics to help readers understand both
current events and the background that produced those events.

Over the more than twenty years of nonfiction lists, the topics have
changed as the world has changed. The lists reflect concerns about contemporary problems and a need to find solutions to those problems.

Ain't Gonna Study War No More: The Story of America's Peace Seekers, Milton Meltzer (1985), 1988

> A chronicle of resistance to war and violence in America's history, this work tells the story of passionate believers in peace who often forfeit their reputations and livelihoods for those beliefs.

Alistair Cooke's America, Alistair Cooke (1973), 1976, 1982

> Based on the popular PBS television series, this lavishly illustrated book presents an Englishman's refreshing view of his adopted country's history.

All the President's Men, Carl Bernstein and Bob Woodward (1974), 1994

> Following lead after lead, two *Washington Post* reporters lift the veil of secrecy surrounding the Nixon administration's Watergate cover-up.

Always Running: La Vida Loca, Gang Days in L.A., Luis Rodriguez (1993), 1994

> Socioeconomic causes breed contemporary gang violence in Los Angeles.

American Dilemma: The Negro Problem and Modern Democracy, Gunnar Myrdal (1962), 1971

> This classic study of the African Americans in America by a social economist becomes also a critical evaluation of American civilization as a whole.

American Political Tradition and the Men Who Made It, Richard Hofstadter (1948), 1971

> Incisive essays interpret the historical significance of such figures as Jefferson, Lincoln, Wilson, Hoover, and Franklin Delano Roosevelt.

Among Schoolchildren, Tracy Kidder (1989), 1991

> An elementary teacher tells about the children and events during one school year.

Amusing Ourselves to Death: Public Discourse in the Age of Show Business, Neil Postman (1985), 1988

> The author believes the act and art of public discourse are being degraded by television, which turns important issues into mass media entertainment.

Anasazi: Ancient People of the Rock, David Muench and Donald G. Pike (1976), 1991

> Archeological evidence and the written records of Spanish explorers reveal the history of an ancient people.

And the Band Played On: Politics, People, and the AIDS Epidemic, Randy Shilts (1987), 1991

> A reporter takes a detailed look at the first five years of the unfolding AIDS epidemic.

Apartheid in Crisis, Mark A. Uhlig (ed.) (1986), 1988

> The various South African factions reveal their attitudes and take their stands.

Arctic Dreams: Imagination and Desire in a Northern Landscape, Barry Lopez (1986), 1988

> Real life and dreams of the Arctic land, its animals, and its people are celebrated.

Art as Image and Idea, Edmund Burke Feldman (1967), 1971

> The functions, styles, and structure of art; the interaction of medium and meaning; and lastly, the problems of art criticism.

Ascent of Man, Jacob Bronowski (1973), 1976, 1982, 1988

> A scientist's history of the human mind and the human condition.

Backlash: The Undeclared War against American Women, Susan Faludi (1991), 1994

> Faludi offers an unflinching analysis of the current status of American women.

Barbarians at the Gate: The Fall of RJR Nabisco, Bryan Burrough and John Helyar (1990), 1994

> Wall Street's largest takeover reveals greed, deceit, and clever maneuvers.

Battle Cry of Freedom: The Civil War Era, James M. McPherson (1988), 1994

> From the Mexican War to Appomattox, the political, military, and economic aspects of the Civil War are examined.

Before the Mayflower: A History of the Negro in America, 1619–1964, Lerone Bennett (1962), 1976

> From the African past, through slavery, wars, and reconstructions— the dramatic story of the African Americans' sojourn in North America.

Being Born, Sheila Kitzinger (1986), 1991

> Intrauterine photographs explain the wonders of gestation and birth.

Best and the Brightest, David Halberstam (1972), 1994

> Kennedy-Johnson intellectuals orchestrate American foreign policy in Indochina.

Bloods: An Oral History of the Vietnam War, Black Veterans and Terry Wallace (ed.) (1984), 1988

> During the Vietnam War, the African American soldiers endured a higher percentage of casualties and returned to a higher percentage of unemployment than any other ethnic group.

Blue Highways: A Journey into America, William Least Heat Moon (1983), 1988

> Traveling miles along the small back roads of the United States allows the author to introduce a series of diverse and unique Americans.

Bones of Contention: Controversies in the Search for Human Origin, Roger Lewin (1988), 1991

> The description of a series of episodes in paleoanthropology brings to light the ongoing debate about the origin of humans.

Borrowing Time: Growing Up with Juvenile Diabetes, Pat Covelli (1979), 1982

> A first-person account of taking responsibility for one's own survival.

Bradshaw on the Family: A Revolutionary Way of Self-Discovery, John Bradshaw (1988), 1991

> By focusing on family problems such as guilt and codependency, Bradshaw helps the reader to grow and change.

Break-Up: The Core of Modern Art, Katherine Kuh (1965), 1976

> Analyzes examples of modern art in terms of the attempt to present life in its structural elements rather than its wholeness.

Brief History of Time: From the Big Bang to Black Holes, Stephen W. Hawking (1988), 1991, 1994

> A very complex subject, cosmology becomes understandable as the author discusses the origin, evolution, and fate of our universe.

Bright Shining Lie: John Paul Vann and America in Vietnam, Neil Sheehan (1988), 1994

> Focusing on corruption, John Paul Vann exposes the undermining of American efforts in the Vietnam War.

Brighter than a Thousand Suns: A Personal History of the Atomic Scientists, Robert Jungk (1958), 1976, 1982

> This vivid account of the development of the atomic bomb achieves continuing relevance by focusing on the moral and psychological problems related to weapons research.

Broken Cord, Michael Dorris (1989), 1994

> Dorris shares the triumphs and difficulties of life with his adopted child, a victim of fetal alcohol syndrome.

Bully for Brontosaurus: Reflections in Natural History, Stephen Jay Gould (1991), 1994

> Essays offer thoughts on evolution and other scientific principles.

Bury My Heart at Wounded Knee: An Indian History of the American West, Dee Brown (1971), 1976, 1982, 1988, 1994

> A narrative of the white man's conquest of the American land as the Native American victims experienced it.

Changing Bodies, Changing Lives: A Book for Teens on Sex and Relationships, Ruth Bell (1982), 1982, 1988

> A direct, thorough, and explicit guide for young adults concerning both physical and emotional aspects of sexuality.

Chaos: Making a New Science, James Gleick (1987), 1994

> Gleick chronicles the development of chaos, the complex new science.

China Men, Maxine Hong Kingston (1980), 1991

> A description of the lives of several generations of Chinese males contributes to an understanding of the experiences of Chinese immigrants.

Civilisation: A Personal View, Kenneth Clark (1970), 1971

> Clark explores history through the works, impulses, and beliefs of the great creative individuals of Western civilization.

Closing of the American Mind, Allan Bloom (1987), 1991

> The author maintains Western civilization is in crisis because its intellectual tradition has been abandoned.

Cognitive Computer: On Language, Learning, and Artificial Intelligence, Roger C. Schank with Peter G. Childers (1984), 1988

> Artificial intelligence experts put computers into perspective and indicate future uses, especially in education.

Common Ground: A Turbulent Decade in the Lives of Three American Families, J. Anthony Lukas (1985), 1988

> A remarkable, intensive analysis of the lives of three families—one African American, one Irish, and one Yankee—who clash in the violent climate of prejudice and racism that erupted in the 1968 Boston school integration crisis.

Complete Book of Pregnancy and Childbirth, Sheila Kitzinger (1980), 1991

> Here's everything you need to know about the emotional and physical changes that occur during the first nine months of human life.

Conduct Unbecoming: Gays and Lesbians in the U.S. Military, Randy Shilts (1993), 1994

>Shilts discusses the contributions and conflicts of gays and lesbians serving in the American armed forces.

Constitution: Reflection of a Changing Nation, Margot Mabie (1986), 1991

>The Constitution of the United States is a living document that adapts to changes in our history.

Control of Nature, John McPhee (1989), 1994

>McPhee turns his attention to Alaska, the last American frontier.

Coping with Date Rape and Acquaintance Rape, Andrea Parrot (1988), 1991

>Both men and women can use these suggested techniques for avoiding date and acquaintance rape.

Cosmos, Carl Sagan (1980), 1982, 1991

>A universal history of the galaxy presents choices for the future.

Crazy to Be Alive in Such a Strange World: Poems about People, Nancy Larrick (ed.) (1977), 1982

>This is a spirited collection of American poetry.

Cultural Literacy: What Every American Needs to Know, E. D. Hirsch Jr. (1987), 1991

>An educated, "culturally literate" member of contemporary American society must understand certain key terms and concepts from history.

Culture and Commitment: The New Relationships between the Generations in the 1970's, Margaret Mead (1970), 1982

>We need not only to recognize global problems, Mead argues, but also to commit ourselves to solving them.

Cycles of Fire: Stars, Galaxies, and the Wonder of Deep Space, William K. Hartman (1988), 1991

>This book explores the formation of stars, the characteristics of the Milky Way, and the possibilities of other worlds in deep space.

Dance of Legislation, Eric Redman (1973), 1976, 1982

>A Senate aide demystifies the legislative process while conveying its attendant drama, frustration, and comedy.

Dark Side of the Marketplace: The Plight of the American Consumer, Warren Magnuson and Jean Carper (1968), 1976

>While Ralph Nader has been the consumer advocate from without, Magnuson has worked within Congress to counter abuses.

Darwin's Century: Evolution and the Men Who Discovered It, Loren Eisely (1958), 1971, 1976, 1982, 1988

> There have been evolutionary theories from the Renaissance to the twentieth century.

Day One: Before Hiroshima and After, Peter Wyden (1985), 1988

> The race to develop the atomic bomb and the aftermath of its first use are covered in this account of the birth of the atomic age.

Death and Life of Great American Cities, Jane Jacobs (1961), 1976

> A witty and passionate defense of the primary role of people in city planning and urban renewal.

Decade of Women: A Ms. History of the Seventies in Words and Pictures, Suzanne Levine and Harriet Lyons (1980), 1982

> Discusses various aspects of women's lives in the 1970s through quotations and photographs.

Democracy in America, Alexis de Tocqueville (1835), 1971, 1976, 1982, 1988

> This classic in political literature examines American society from the viewpoint of a leading French magistrate who visited the United States in 1831.

Desert Smells like Rain: A Naturalist in Papago Indian Country, Gary Paul Nabhan (1982), 1994

> Nature plays a vital part in Papago Indian culture.

Devil in the Shape of a Woman: Witchcraft in Colonial New England, Carol F. Karlsen (1987), 1994

> The status of women in colonial society affects the Salem witch accusations.

Distant Mirror: The Calamitous Fourteenth Century, Barbara Wertheim Tuchman (1978), 1994

> Tuchman uses the example of a single feudal lord to trace the history of the fourteenth century.

Do What You Love, the Money Will Follow: Discovering Your Right Livelihood, Marsha Sinetar (1989), 1991

> This New Age self-help manual works with self-esteem and other concepts to develop personal satisfaction in employment and life.

Domestic Revolutions: A Social History of Domestic Family Life, Steven Mintz and Susan Kellogg (1988), 1994

> Is the American family changing its structure and purpose?

Don Coyote: The Good Times and Bad of a Maligned American Original, Dayton O. Hyde (1986), 1991

> A rancher defends the place of coyotes in the environmental scheme of things after rescuing and caring for one of the breed.

Double Helix: A Personal Account of the Discovery of the Structure of DNA, James D. Watson and Guntor S. Stent (ed.) (1968), 1976, 1982, 1988

> The author re-creates the excitement of participating in a momentous discovery and reveals to the nonscientist how the scientific method works.

Dream Is Alive, Barbara Embury with Thomas D. Crouch (1990), 1994

> Join Embury on a typical shuttle flight using photographs from a 1984 mission.

Eight Men Out: The Black Sox and the 1919 World Series, Eliot Asinoff (1963), 1994

> It's all here: the players, the scandal, the shame, and the damage the 1919 World Series caused for America's national pastime.

Essential Writings of Mahatma Gandhi, Iyer Raghaven (ed.) (1991), 1994

> Gandhi discusses the philosophical underpinnings that guided his nonviolent life.

Everything We Had: An Oral History of the Vietnam War by Thirty-three American Soldiers Who Fought It, Al Santoli (ed.) (1981), 1982

> Veterans of the Vietnam War from all branches of the service recount the impact of the war on their lives.

Eyes on the Prize: America's Civil Rights Years 1954–1965, Juan Williams (1987), 1991, 1994

> The "prize" of equal rights for African Americans is closer at hand because of the Civil Rights movement in the United States.

Fate of the Earth, Jonathan Schell (1982), 1988

> The fear of human extinction by a nuclear holocaust is discussed in this profoundly sobering and frightening book.

Favorite Folktales from Around the World, Jane Yolen (ed.) (1986), 1991, 1994

> This collection of wonderful international folktales provides an understanding of the underpinnings of diverse cultures.

Feminine Mystique, Betty Friedan (1963), 1976, 1988

> Many feel that the first edition of this book precipitated the women's liberation movement by inspiring new appraisals of roles and aspirations.

Fifty Simple Things You Can Do to Save the Earth, Earth Works Group (1989), 1991

>   Readers can help to save the earth if they use these suggestions in their daily lives.

Final Harvest: An American Tragedy, Andrew H. Malcolm (1986), 1988

>   A poverty-stricken, uneducated farmer murders the local bank manager who foreclosed on his eighty acres, making both men victims of the painful changes affecting America's agricultural heartland.

Fire in the Lake: The Vietnamese and the Americans in Vietnam, Frances Fitz-Gerald (1989), 1991

>   A knowledge of the history of Vietnam helps readers understand the reasons for the Vietnam War.

Fire Next Time, James Baldwin (1963), 1994

>   Expatriate Baldwin issues a wake-up call to counteract America's racist attitudes.

First Dictionary of Cultural Literacy: What Our Children Need to Know, E. D. Hirsch Jr. (ed.) (1989), 1991

>   Using a dictionary format, hundreds of "windows" reveal what it means to be a "culturally literate," educated American citizen.

First Freedom: The Tumultuous History of Free Speech in America, Nat Hentoff (1980), 1982

>   This historical study of the First Amendment includes important court cases.

Five Senses, F. Gonzales-Crussi (1989), 1991

>   Constant repetition on the human senses leads the author into a remembrance of his past.

Friendly Shakespeare: A Thoroughly Painless Guide to the Best of the Bard, Norrie Epstein (1993), 1994

>   Gain a perspective of Shakespeare's works through these sidelights, interpretations, anecdotes, and historical insights.

Future Shock, Alvin Toffler (1970), 1976

>   This book stimulates discussion of the effects of rapidly accelerating change in our society.

Gateway to History, Allan Nevins (1938), 1971

>   Nevins defines the scope and variety of the field of history and outlines his views on history's objectives, both as a science and as an art.

Getting It Down: How to Put Your Ideas on Paper, Judi Kesselman-Turkel and Franklynn Peterson (1983), 1991

> This manual can help organize your ideas into a well-planned, clearly written presentation.

Gideon's Trumpet, Anthony Lewis (1964), 1994

> One determined convict changes the American legal system.

Girl, Interrupted, Susanna Kaysen (1993), 1994

> Kaysen provides unique insight into mental illness.

Glory and the Dream: A Narrative History of America, 1932–1972, William Manchester (1974), 1982

> From major calamities to minor trivia, this remarkable exploration celebrates modern America in a spirited, lively narrative.

Goddesses in Everywoman: A New Psychology of Women, Jean Shinoda Bolen (1985), 1991

> Women have many roles in contemporary everyday life.

Gödel, Escher, Bach: An Eternal Golden Braid, Douglas R. Hofstadter (1979), 1982

> Math, computers, art, music, and puzzles combined in a "fugue on minds and machines."

Gods in Everyman: A New Psychology of Men's Lives and Loves, Jean Shinoda Bolen (1989), 1991

> Psychological analysis demonstrates that men display certain traits that are similar to the archetypes of Greek gods.

Gods, Graves, and Scholars: The Story of Archaeology, C. W. Ceram (1967), 1971, 1976, 1982, 1988

> This work reviews archaeological discoveries of the last two centuries—in Pompeii, Troy, Crete, Egypt, Assyria, Babylonia, Sumeria, and the Yucatan—and introduces the people who made them.

Good Neighbors? The United States and Latin America, Ann E. Weiss (1985), 1988

> The ongoing, complex relationship between the United States and Latin America is presented in an easy-to-read style.

Gorillas in the Mist, Dian Fossey (1983), 1991

> Observing and defending the endangered mountain gorilla in Africa became Dian Fossey's life work and her obsession.

Graphic History of Architecture, John Mansbridge (1967), 1971

> The three-dimensional form and dynamic construction of buildings are shown through plans, elevations, cutaways, and isometric drawings in a way unmatched by words or photographs.

Great Expectations: America and the Baby Boom Generation, Landon Y. Jones (1980), 1982

> Being part of the largest generation in American history has its strengths and its problems.

Greenhouse Effect, Kathlyn Gay (1986), 1991

> Rising levels of carbon dioxide in the atmosphere are causing changes in the earth's climate.

Growing Up Asian American: An Anthology, Maria Hong (ed.) (1993), 1994

> Asian American authors are featured in this literary collection focused on growing up.

Guinness Book of Records 1492: The World Five Hundred Years Ago, Deborah Manley (ed.) (1992), 1994

> Discover the world as it was more than five hundred years ago.

Hiroshima, John Hersey (1946), 1988, 1994

> John Hersey comes to Hiroshima, Japan, in 1946 to report on the first city to be destroyed by an atomic bomb and returns forty years later to tell what happened since his first visit.

History of Art and Music, H. W. Janson and Joseph Kerman (1960), 1971

> This book offers a panoramic history of art and music in the Western world.

History of Western Philosophy, Bertrand Russell (1945), 1971

> Philosophy emerges as "an integral part of social and political life; not as the isolated speculations of remarkable individuals, but as both an effect and a cause of the character of the various communities in which different systems flourish."

Holy Bible: New Revised Standard Version, (1973), 1991

> Biblical scholars revise text and modernize terms to bring one version of the Bible up-to-date.

Hometown Heroes: Successful Deaf Youth in America, Diane Robinette (1990), 1994

> These profiles show handicapped youth succeeding in today's world.

How Does a Poem Mean, John Ciardi (1960), 1971, 1976

> A poet and critic discusses the value and nature of poetry, using selections from six centuries of American and English poems.

How the World Was One: Beyond the Global Village, Arthur C. Clarke (1992), 1994

> International telecommunications are changing the way we view ourselves and our world.

How to Get Started When You Don't Know Where to Begin, Patricia Hoyt (1980), 1982

> Issues such as renting an apartment, opening a checking account, doing the laundry, and other practical situations are addressed.

Hunter's Stew and Hangtown Fry: What Pioneer Americans Ate and Why, Lila Perl (1979), 1991

> The food choices of early pioneers continue to influence what we eat in various parts of the country.

Ideas and Men: The Story of Western Thought, Crane Brinton (1950), 1971

> This work presents an analysis of the major ideas and concepts that have helped to shape the course of Western civilization.

Imperial Presidency, M. Arthur Schlesinger (1973), 1976, 1982

> Power has been used and abused by American presidents.

In Search of Excellence: Lessons from America's Best Run Companies, Thomas J. Peters and Robert H. Waterman Jr. (1982), 1991

> Consultants identify forty-two companies and tell why they are successful.

In Search of Meaning, Living Religions of the World, Carl Voss (1968), 1971

> The history and origins of the great religions, including their spiritual, cultural, and ethical values.

In Suspect Terrain, John McPhee (1983), 1991

> The glaciers that moved through the northeastern states formed and shaped the land as we know it today.

In the Shadow of Man, Jane Goodall (1983), 1991

> Goodall describes the chimpanzee group she studied in the Gombe Stream Chimpanzee Reserve in Tanzania.

Intimate Play: Creating Romance in Everyday Life, William Betcher (1987), 1991

> These playful strategies may help you bond with family and friends, spouses or partners.

Invisible Men: Life in Baseball's Negro Leagues, Donn Rogosin (1983), 1994

> The great Negro League players finally gain recognition for their contributions to baseball.

Johnstown Flood, David McCullough (1968), 1994

> McCullough shares the story behind one of America's most devastating natural disasters.

Joy of Music, Leonard Bernstein (1959), 1971, 1994

>   Bernstein presents a fresh and enthusiastic approach to the "joy of music."

Keepers of the Earth: Native American Stories and Environmental Activities for Children, Michael J. Caduto and Joseph Bruchac (1988), 1991

>   This manual provides insights into the Native American world through stories, recipes, and outdoor activities.

Language of Cities, Fran P. Hosken (1968), 1971

>   An architect and city planner shows how cities are places of scale and space, light and shadow, color and texture, form and movement.

Last Chance to See, Douglas Adams and Mark Cowardine (1991), 1994

>   Adams delivers a humorous, touching view of his travels to find endangered species around the world.

Laying Waste: The Poisoning of America by Toxic Chemicals, Michael H. Brown (1980), 1982, 1988

>   The improper disposal of toxic chemicals in the Love Canal area of Niagara Falls, N. Y., is one of many situations chronicled in this book, which serves as a call to action on a serious environmental problem.

Learning to Look: A Handbook for the Visual Arts, Joshua C. Taylor (1957), 1971, 1976

>   A clear, concrete explanation of what to look for in art.

Legends, Lies, and Cherished Myths of World History, Richard Shenkman (1993), 1994

>   Legends, myths, and lies reveal history's errors with humor.

Let Us Now Praise Famous Men, James Agee and Walker Evans (1960), 1976, 1982, 1988

>   Agee and Evans portray three tenant farmer families at the depths of the depression in words and photographs that are perhaps closer to art than to commentary.

Licit and Illicit Drugs: The Consumers Union Report, Edward M. Brecher and Consumer Reports Editors (1972), 1982

>   An authoritative reference work about drugs used in the United States.

Lives of a Cell: Notes of a Biology Watcher, Lewis Thomas (1974), 1976, 1982, 1988

>   Looking through a microscope at the tiniest forms of life, Thomas discerns in their interrelationships clues to the mystery of life.

Living by the Word: Selected Writings 1973–1987, Alice Walker (1988), 1994

> Walker's essays on race, politics, women, and life are collected in this volume.

Living Planet: A Portrait of the Earth, David Attenborough (1984), 1994

> Various habitats expand the vision of planet Earth.

Loch Ness Monster: Opposing Viewpoints, Robert D. San Souci (1989), 1991

> The presentation of diverse viewpoints allows the reader to form independent judgments about "Nessie."

Lonely Days Were Sundays: Reflections of a Jewish Southerner, Eli Evans (1993), 1994

> A Jewish Southerner shares his reflections on his life and society.

Lucy: The Beginnings of Human Kind, Donald C. Johanson and Maitland A. Edey (1980), 1982, 1988

> An account of the discovery of a 3.5-million-year-old prehuman skeleton and its impact on the study of our ancestors.

Mainstreams of Modern Art, John Canaday (1959), 1971

> The art editor of the *New York Times* examines art from David to Picasso, discussing classicism, romanticism, and realism.

Making of a Counter Culture: Reflections on the Technocratic Society and Its Youthful Opposition, Theodore Roszak (1969), 1976

> The influence of such personalities as Herbert Marcuse, Allen Ginsberg, Timothy Leary, and Paul Goodman are examined together with the leading causes of youthful dissent in the sixties.

Man and His Symbols, Carl Gustav Jung (1964), 1991, 1994

> A psychiatrist introduces the concept of the collective unconscious.

Mathematics in Western Culture, Morris Kline (1953), 1976

> Kline explores the role of mathematics as it relates to other disciplines.

Maus: A Survivor's Tale, Art Spiegelman (1986), 1994

> Spiegelman details his father's view of the Holocaust in a graphic format.

Maus II: Here My Troubles Began, Art Spiegelman (1991), 1994

> Spiegelman continues his graphic novel story about his father and the Holocaust.

Measure of Our Success: A Letter to My Children and Yours, Marian Wright Edelman (1992), 1994

> A child advocate shares her thoughts on values, raising families, and the future of our country.

Media Sexploitation, Wilson Bryan Key (1977), 1991

> A look at the complex world of advertising reveals the way consumers are led to make purchases based on imagery.

Medical Detectives, Berton Roueche (1984), 1991

> Scientists, doctors, and epidemiologists work to discover the causes of many different diseases.

Megatrends: Ten New Directions Transforming Our Lives, John Naisbitt (1983), 1988

> Naisbitt investigates the societal changes of the 1980s.

Men of Mathematics, Eric T. Bell (1937), 1961, 1963, 1965, 1968, 1994

> The lives and achievements of world-renowned mathematicians are told with wit and good humor.

Millennium: Tribal Wisdom and the Modern World, Davi Maybury-Lewis (1992), 1994

> Maybury-Lewis profiles members of several tribal cultures.

Minding the Body, Mending the Mind, Joan Borysenko (1987), 1991

> Borysenko presents an integrated approach to healing based on meditation, diet, anxiety release, exercise, and relaxation.

Miracle at Philadelphia: The Story of the Constitutional Convention, May to September, 1787, Catherine Drinker Bowen (1986), 1988

> The historic formation of the Constitution is recounted in this day-by-day report of the debates and compromises that took place in Philadelphia.

Miracle of Language, Richard Lederer (1991), 1994

> Words are often used incorrectly, and the results can be humorous.

Modern Times: The World from the Twenties to the Eighties, Paul Johnson (1983), 1988

> A fascinating presentation of world history and politics is combined with thought-provoking critical interpretation.

Mothers of Invention: From the Bra to the Bomb: Forgotten Women and Their Unforgettable Ideas, Ethlie A. Vare and Greg Ptacek (1988), 1994

> Women inventors overcome obstacles.

Move Your Shadow: South Africa Black and White, Joseph Lelyveld (1985), 1988, 1991

> From a personal point of view, the author describes the South African conflict.

My Soul Is Rested: Movement Days in the Deep South Remembered, Howell Raines (1983), 1988

> The gathering force of the Civil Rights movement, from the Montgomery bus boycott of 1955 to the death of Martin Luther King Jr. in 1968, as told by the men and women who remember the glory and tragedy of those days.

Mythology, Edith Hamilton (1942), 1971, 1976, 1982, 1988

> Gods and heroes, their clashes and adventures, come alive in this splendid retelling of the Greek, Roman, and Norse myths.

Never to Forget: The Jews of the Holocaust, Milton Meltzer (1976), 1982, 1988

> This book "is an act of mourning and a call to remember," so that history will not be repeated.

New Industrial State, John Kenneth Galbraith (1967), 1971

> Galbraith urges that we drastically re-examine our concepts of the marketplace, the state, public versus private, and the impact of large corporations on our times.

New Our Bodies, Ourselves, Boston Women's Health Book Collective Staff (1992), 1994

> This revised edition of the 1973 classic examines the total implications of womanhood, from the physical to the psychological.

New World of Philosophy, Abraham Kaplan (1961), 1971, 1976

> Kaplan interprets the main movements in modern philosophic thought, including existentialism, Freudian psychology, Communism, Buddhism, Chinese philosophy, and Zen.

Next Whole Earth Catalog: Access to Tools, Stewart Brand (ed.) (1971), 1982

> Tools aid in the process of education and the shaping of the environment.

Number: The Language of Science, Tobias Dantzig (1954), 1971

> This classic on the history of numbers, "the world's universal language," gives concepts, ideas, and their implementation.

Occupational Outlook Handbook, U.S. Bureau of Labor Statistics (annual), 1991

> This handbook lists qualifications, potential earnings, working conditions, employment trends, and job opportunities for many careers.

Odyssey of Homer: A Modern Translation, Homer (c. 750 B.C.), 1976, 1982

> A Greek epic tells of the adventures of the hero Odysseus during his perilous and protracted journey home from the Trojan War.

On Aggression, Konrad Lorenz (1966), 1971, 1976, 1982, 1988

> A thought-provoking analysis of the fighting instinct in beast and man, which is directed against members of the same species.

On Violence, Hannah Arendt (1970), 1991

> The author explores the reasons why violence is so prevalent in modern society.

One Boy at War: My Life in the AIDS Underground, Paul Sergios (1993), 1994

> Those suffering from AIDS take desperate measures in their efforts to survive.

One Child, Torey L. Hayden (1980), 1982

> A severely abused and emotionally disturbed child gradually realizes her potential with the help of a courageous teacher.

One Two Three—Infinity: Facts and Speculations of Science, George Gamow (1961), 1971

> This collection brings together some of the most interesting facts and theories of modern science.

Operating Manual for Spaceship Earth, R. Buckminster Fuller (1969), 1976, 1982

> The inventor of the geodesic dome admonishes us to consider our planet as a complete environment.

Other America: Poverty in the United States, Michael Harrington (1962), 1971

> This book shocked America into realizing the extent to which its affluence is creating poverty.

Other Lives, Other Selves: A Jungian Psychotherapist Discovers Past Lives, Roger J. Woolger (1987), 1991

> Case studies of reincarnation illuminate theories and strategies.

Our House Divided: Seven Japanese American Families in World War II, Tomi Kaizawa Knaefler (1991), 1994

> The United States is a place of neither shelter nor freedom for Japanese Americans during World War II.

Patterns of Culture, Ruth Fulton Benedict (1961), 1976, 1982

> For a quarter of a century, this book has provided an introduction to the understanding of anthropology.

Pelican History of Psychology, Robert Thomson (1968), 1971

> Psychology had its beginnings in philosophy and evolved through the achievements of Freud, Jung, and others.

Person: His and Her Development throughout the Life Cycle, Theodore Lidz (1968), 1971

> This treatment of personality development moves through fifteen stages, from prebirth to death.

Philosophy: An Introduction, John H. Randall and Justus Buchler (1942), 1971

> The different branches of philosophy—aesthetics, ethics, epistemology, logic, metaphysics, and axiology—are explained.

Planet Earth, Jonathan Weiner (1986), 1991

> This book summarizes current discoveries and current thinking in the earth sciences.

Portable World Bible, Robert O. Ballou (ed.) (1976), 1976, 1982, 1988

> This Bible covers the Hindu, Buddhist, Parsi, Judeo-Christian, Moslem, Confucian, and Taoist religious traditions and includes background information on each.

Power of Myth, Joseph Campbell (1958), 1991, 1994

> Themes and symbols present in our daily lives reflect many world religions and mythologies.

Prisoner without a Name, Cell without a Number, Jacobo Timerman (1981), 1982

> A master journalist recounts his imprisonment and torture in an Argentine prison and speaks out for human rights.

Race: How Blacks and Whites Think and Feel about the American Obsession, Studs Terkel (1992), 1994

> Interviews uncover the full range of America's views on racial issues.

Rachel and Her Children: Homeless Families in America, Jonathan Kozol (1988), 1991

> Men, women, and children who are residents of a hotel for the homeless in New York discuss their predicament.

La Raza: The Mexican Americans, Stan Steiner (1970), 1971, 1991

> A study of the problems of "the Race," which includes an account of the journey of Cesar Chavez from the boyhood of a migrant farmworker to the role of leader of his people.

Rescue: The Story of How Gentiles Saved Jews in the Holocaust, Milton Meltzer (1988), 1991, 1994

> Many people risk their lives to save others during the Holocaust.

Right Stuff, Tom Wolfe (1983), 1988

> This inside story reveals the glory and exploitation that attended the selection, training, and flight of America's first astronauts.

Road Less Traveled, M. Scott Peck (1985), 1991

> An exploration of the nature of love relationships and ways that psychiatry and religion enrich our lives.

Sand County Almanac, Aldo Leopold (1949), 1994

> Leopold shares his present and future visions of a natural world.

Savage Inequalities: Children in America's Schools, Jonathan Kozol (1991), 1994

> Kozol advocates equalizing per pupil school expenditures in America's public schools.

Sea around Us, Rachel Carson (1951), 1971

> This scientific and poetic account reveals the changes in the sea that began more than 2 billion years ago, as well as explorations and important developments in oceanographic research.

Season Ticket: A Baseball Companion, Roger Angell (1988), 1994

> A veteran sports writer profiles the sport's 1983–87 seasons.

Should Drugs Be Legalized?, Susan Neiburg Terkel (1990), 1994

> Following an overview of drug use in the United States, Terkel discusses the regulation of illegal drugs.

Silent Spring, Rachel Carson (1962), 1976, 1988, 1994

> Carson raises the first warnings about the destruction of the environment.

Small Victories: The Real World of a Teacher, Her Students, and Their High School, Samuel C. Freedman (1990), 1994

> How does this overcrowded, underfunded school send 92 percent of its graduates on to higher education?

Soul on Ice, Eldridge Cleaver (1968), 1994

> Through essays and open letters written while in prison, Cleaver expresses the inner feelings and drives of the outraged African American man.

Souls of Black Folk: Essays and Sketches, W. E. B. Du Bois (1903), 1994

> Educator Du Bois describes the lives and history of African American farmers, including the career of Booker T. Washington.

Space, Time and Architecture, Siegfried Giedion (1967), 1971

> A fundamental text illuminates the interrelation of materials, techniques, and human needs in terms of architectural design and city planning.

Sportsmedicine Book, Gabe Mirkin and Marshall Hoffman (1978), 1982

> Sports medicine focuses on physical and psychological effects of physical activity, with emphasis on preventing injury.

Stephen Hawking's Universe, John Boslough (1984), 1991

> Hawking presents his theories on the universe in general, and black holes in particular.

Story of Philosophy, William J. Durant (1926), 1976, 1982, 1988

> Certain personalities dominate the story of philosophy.

Strange Career of Jim Crow, Comer Vann Woodward (1957), 1976

> The effects of Southern segregation laws and of the aftermath of the Civil Rights movement in both the North and South are analyzed.

Strange Footprints on the Land: Vikings in America, Constance H. Frick Irwin (1980), 1991

> Historians perform unusual detective work to solve the mystery of the Viking influence in pre-Columbia America.

Summerhill: A Radical Approach to Child Rearing, Alexander Sutherland Neill (1960), 1976

> A famous experimental school where freedom and nonrepression create a different kind of learning environment is described.

Taking on the Press: Constitutional Rights in Conflict, Melvyn Bernard Zerman (1986), 1988

> Freedom of the press is examined through a discussion of landmark cases that cause controversy over whose rights should prevail.

Terrorism: A Special Kind of Violence, Margaret Oldroyd Hyde and Elizabeth H. Forsyth (1987), 1991

> The authors explore the origin of terrorism and discuss the political, religious, and psychological implications of this type of violence.

Theory of Literature, Rene Wellek and Austin Warren (1949), 1971

> This theory of criticism examines the nature, functions, form, and contents of literature, rather than the environment that influences its creations.

There Are No Children Here: The Story of Two Boys Growing Up in the Other America, Alex Kotlowitz (1991), 1994

> Two young boys struggle to survive in one of Chicago's worst housing projects.

There Is a River: The Black Struggle for Freedom in America, Vincent Harding (1981), 1982, 1988

> African Americans from the first captives in Africa to the end of the Civil War rebel against slavery.

Thinking Out Loud: On the Personal, the Political, the Public, and the Private, Anna Quindlen (1993), 1994

> Op-ed pieces from the *New York Times* underscore Quindlen's thoughts on human rights, abortion, and justice.

Third Wave, Alvin Toffler (1980), 1982

> A futuristic look at what Toffler perceives to be civilization's imminent entrance into a new age of social development.

Thirty Days to a More Powerful Vocabulary, Wilfred John Funk and Norman Lewis (1988), 1991

> The English vocabulary of educated people can be mastered with these useful techniques.

Thunder on the Right: The New Right and the Politics of Resentment, Alan Crawford (1980), 1982

> A conservative explores the dangers of the New Right, its leaders, and its groups.

To Bear Any Burden: The Vietnam War and Its Aftermath in the Words of Americans and Southeast Asians, Al Santoli (1985), 1988

> The Vietnam War's origins and its aftermath come alive through interviews with American civilians and military personnel as well as Southeast Asians.

Today's Isms: Communism, Fascism, Capitalism, Socialism, William Ebenstein and Edwin Fogelman (1985), 1971, 1976, 1982, 1988

> The authors provide an approach to various social systems and analyze the psychological appeal of each.

True Believer: Thoughts on the Nature of Mass Movements, Eric Hoffer (1951), 1976

> Hoffer analyzes fanaticism, nationalism, and other "isms" in terms of the psychology of mass movements.

Twelve Years a Slave, Solomon Northrup (1968), 1994

> A free man is kidnapped and sold into slavery.

Two Cultures, C. P. Snow (1964), 1971

> A scientist who is also a successful novelist discusses the split between art and science.

Two Old Women: An Alaska Legend of Betrayal, Courage and Survival, Velma Wallis (1993), 1994

> Two old Athabaskan women, abandoned by their tribe, discover the strength to survive.

Understanding Media: The Extensions of Man, Marshall McLuhan (1964), 1976

> McLuhan suggests a study of the media as a means for better perception of our environment and our relationship to it.

Unforgettable Fire: Pictures Drawn by Atomic Bomb Survivors, Japan Broadcasting Corp. (ed.) (1981), 1982

> Survivors of Hiroshima draw more than one hundred pictures.

Vietnam: A History, Stanley Karnow (1983), 1994

> Karnow covers more than two centuries of armed conflict in Vietnam.

Violence! Our Fastest Growing Public Health Problem, John Langone (1984), 1988

> The violence in our homes, streets, prisons, and sports arenas is examined to provide insight into the underlying causes and possible solutions to this serious social problem.

Walden (1854) and **Civil Disobedience** (1849), Henry David Thoreau, 1976, 1982

> Thoreau celebrates nature and independence.

Walk across America, Peter Jenkins (1979), 1982

> A personal account of one man's efforts to understand his own life within the context of life around him as he takes a walking journey from Connecticut to New Orleans.

War Clouds in the West: Indians and Cavalrymen, 1860–1890, Albert Marrin (1984), 1991

> Native Americans fight to survive in the late nineteenth century when increasing numbers of pioneers settle on their land.

Way of Love, a Way of Life: A Young Person's Introduction to What It Means to Be Gay, Frances Hanckel and John Cunningham (1979), 1982

> This positive guide to what being homosexual means—physically, emotionally, and socially—is presented through photographs, interviews, and personal histories.

Way Things Work, David Macaulay (1989), 1991

> By dealing with basic principles, the author relates how approximately 350 machines function.

Way to Cook, Julia Child (1989), 1991

> An advocate of fine food and good eating presents French and American cooking styles and recipes.

We the People: An Atlas of America's Ethnic Diversity, James Paul Allen and Eugene James Turner (1988), 1991

> Maps show the ethnic makeup of the American population.

What Is Sociology: An Introduction to the Discipline and Profession, Alex Inkeles (1964), 1971

> Inkeles reviews the issues facing sociology and the many varying methods, interpretations, and conceptions of man and social processes.

What to Listen For in Music, Aaron Copland (1939), 1976

> The composer provides a basic introduction to the mysteries of musical composition and music appreciation based on a series of lectures.

What's Happening to My Body? Book for Boys: A Growing Up Guide for Parents and Sons, Lynda Madaras and Area Madaras (1987), 1991

> Here's detailed information about male bodies as they change and mature.

What's Happening to My Body? Book for Girls: A Growing Up Guide for Parents and Daughters, Lynda Madaras and Area Madaras (1987), 1991

> Here's detailed information about female bodies as they change and mature.

Who's to Know? Information, the Media and Public Awareness, Ann E. Weiss (1990), 1994

> Who decides what's reported on TV and in the papers?

Working: People Talk about What They Do All Day and How They Feel about What They Do, Studs Terkel (1974), 1976, 1982

> Terkel interviews an industrial spy, a jockey, a nurse, and many others who reveal that the American feeling for work ranges from utter indifference to total commitment.

World History, William McNeil (1967), 1971

> McNeil provides a comprehensive history of the world.

World Must Know: The History of the Holocaust as Told in the United States Holocaust Memorial Museum, U.S. Holocaust Museum (1994), 1994

>   This history covers both the persecuted and the persecutors of the Holocaust.

Worldly Philosophers: The Lives, Times and Ideas of the Great Economic Thinkers, Robert L. Heilbroner (1961), 1971, 1976, 1982, 1988

>   The lives and doctrines of David Ricardo, the Utopians, Karl Marx, Thorstein Veblen, and John Maynard Keynes are explored.

Yen! Japan's New Financial Empire and Its Threat to America, Daniel Burstein (1988), 1991

>   An analysis of Japanese corporate politics reveals the influence of Japanese business on the global economy.

Youngest Science: Notes of a Medicine Watcher, Lewis Thomas (1991), 1994

>   A single lifetime serves as the framework for this history of medicine.

Now/Current

Many of us have a vague "feeling" that things are moving faster. Doctors and executives alike complain that they cannot keep up with the latest developments in their fields . . . Among many there is an uneasy mood—a suspicion that change is out of control.

from *Future Shock* by Alvin Toffler

In 1971 and 1976 the Outstanding Books for the College Bound Committee decided to choose a group of books that especially reflected the turbulent and exciting events that were taking place in the late sixties and early seventies. The books selected were published in separate brochures. In 1971 the title was "Outstanding Books on the Now Scene," and in 1976 it was "Outstanding Books on the Current Scene." The introduction to both lists read as follows:

The books on this list present a broad coverage of ideas, interests, and problems that express the social and personal concerns of today's young adults.

Unlike other lists, no attempt was made to divide the books into genres. Fiction, nonfiction, poetry (more here than on any other lists), and biography live side by side. The thread that ties these books together is the sense that during the late sixties and early seventies enormous changes were taking place, and there were books being published that provided special insight and explanation. These books will provide readers with an understanding of a time that altered traditional concepts with an impact that shook the world. The aftershocks are still being felt.

Alive: The Story of the Andes Survivors, Piers Paul Read (1974), 1976

Plane crash victims in the Andes, facing subzero temperatures and no food, are forced to make a decision—eat their dead comrades or die themselves.

All the President's Men, Carl Bernstein and Bob Woodward (1974), 1976

Following lead after lead, two *Washington Post* reporters lift the veil of secrecy surrounding the Nixon administration's Watergate cover-up

Andromeda Strain, Michael Crichton (1969), 1971

Four scientists must race against time to isolate a deadly microorganism from outer space that has killed all but two in a small Arizona town.

Astrologer, John Cameron (1972), 1976

By using natal configurations, computers predict malignant and benign potentials of each human birth and are able to herald a Catholic messiah and a "perfect" world.

Autobiography of Malcolm X, Malcolm X (1965), 1971

A revealing, personal account of life in the ghetto, in prison, and as a Black Muslim.

Bell Jar, Sylvia Plath (1963), 1976

No longer able to cope with her feelings of inferiority, Esther Greenwood, a talented college junior, retreats to the protective cover of the bell jar.

Bermuda Triangle Mystery Solved, Larry Kusche (1975), 1976

Expert sleuthing and research blast the supernatural explanations for the disappearance of ships, planes, and men within this area of the Atlantic.

Between Myth and Morning: Women Awakening, Elizabeth Janeway (1974), 1976

Believing that the women's movement was inevitable, this journalist explores ways to ensure that women are viewed as equals, not just as "helpmates."

Biological Time Bomb, Gordon Rattray Taylor (1968), 1971

In the offing are memory-erasing drugs, choice of gender in the offspring, reconstructed organisms, and the indefinite postponement of death.

Black Rage, William H. Grier and Price M. Cobbs (1968), 1976

Two African American psychiatrists tell why African Americans are angry—why some are so angry that they are "compelled to burn, loot, and kill in a rage against white society."

Blackthink: My Life as a Black Man and White Man, Jesse Owens (1970), 1971

Owens argues for dealing with people as individuals and feels that too much concentration on African American studies and "black rage" is overreaction, serving to perpetuate racism.

Bless the Beasts and Children, Glendon Swarthout (1970), 1971

Five misfits in an Arizona boys' camp sneak out on a daring escapade to save a herd of buffalo from bloodthirsty, gun-toting tourists.

Body Language, Julius Fast (1970), 1976

One's body unconsciously expresses feelings and emotions.

Brain Changers: Scientists and the New Mind Control, Maya Pines (1973), 1976

The fact that the mind can be improved or impaired by modern scientific methods has created moral and social dilemmas for modern man.

Buried Alive: The Biography of Janis Joplin, Myra Friedman (1973), 1976

Although adored by her loyal audiences, Janis Joplin is plagued by loneliness and insecurity and seeks an "out" in alcohol and drugs.

Carrying the Fire: An Astronaut's Journeys, Michael Collins (1974), 1976

Mike Collins, astronaut, writes an intelligent, technical, yet personal and breezy account of the education of a space man and what it's like "up there."

Catch-22, Joseph Heller (1969), 1971

A broad comedy confronting the humbug and hypocrisy of war and mass society as Captain Yossarian frantically attempts to stay alive despite endless bombing missions.

Chocolate War, Robert Cormier (1974), 1976

When Jerry refuses to sell chocolates for a fund-raising drive, he upsets the power structure of his school and becomes the object of a "war" of intimidation and violence.

Choice: The Issue of Black Survival in America, Samuel F. Yette (1971), 1976

The former *Newsweek* Washington correspondent presents evidence that there is a concerted effort in this country to re-enslave, perhaps even to wipe out, the African American.

Closing Circle, Barry Commoner (1972), 1976

> Professor Commoner warns that we are the unknowing victims of smog, nitrate, and waste pollution caused by shortsighted technology and the relentless drive for profits.

Culture and Commitment: The New Relationships between the Generations in the 1970's, Margaret Mead (1970), 1971, 1976

> We need not only to recognize global problems, Mead argues, but also to commit ourselves to solving them.

Custer Died for Your Sins: An Indian Manifesto, Vine Deloria Jr. (1969), 1971, 1976

> The author, himself a Standing Rock Sioux, destroys the historical and contemporary misconceptions of Native Americans and discusses the many problems facing them today.

Daybreak, Joan Baez (1968), 1971

> An evocative, fragmented, informal autobiography of the folksinging spokeswoman for civil liberties and nonviolent resistance.

Death Is a Noun: A View of the End of Life, John Langone (1972), 1976

> "Is abortion murder?" "When is a person dead?" and other moral questions are considered objectively in this "view of the end of life."

Drug Scene, Donald B. Louria (1968), 1971

> The illicit use of dangerous drugs will remain a problem until "this society regains its vigor, direction and integrity."

Dummy, Ernest Tidyman (1974), 1976

> A poor African American, Donald Lang, who could not hear, talk, or write, was tried and convicted for the murder of a prostitute purely on circumstantial evidence.

Each Other's Victims, Milton Travers (1970), 1971

> Father and son grapple to understand themselves and each other in this graphic account of life in the drug culture.

Eating May Be Hazardous to Your Health, How Your Government Fails to Protect You from the Dangers in Your Food, Jacqueline Verrett and Jean Carper (1974), 1976

> Arguing that the Federal Drug Administration does not protect the public, the authors describe chemicals added to popular foods that have caused cancer, malformed children, and other tragedies.

Environmental Handbook, Garrett De Bell (comp.) (1970), 1971

> The planet Earth needs help! This handbook suggests action that can be taken in any community, by any individual.

Escape from Childhood, John Holt (1974), 1976

> Holt argues that the rights and responsibilities of adult citizens be made available to any young person, of whatever age, who wants to make use of them.

Festival! The Book of American Musical Celebrations, Jerry Hopkins (1970), 1971

> From the mid-fifties to Woodstock and Big Sur, the successes and failures, the togetherness and excitement of "happenings" are conveyed through text and photographs.

Fixer, Bernard Malamud (1966), 1971

> Victim of a vicious anti-Semitic conspiracy, Yakov Bok is in a Russian prison, with only his indomitable will to sustain him.

Foxfire Book, Eliot Wigginton (ed.) (1972), 1976

> Students from Appalachia are turned off by school until a teacher involves them in their heritage—folklore, mountain crafts, and natural medicine—and encourages them to write about it.

Future Shock, Alvin Toffler (1970), 1971

> This book stimulates discussion of the effects of rapidly accelerating change in our society.

Handbook of Adolescence, Marvin J. Gersch and Iris F. Litt (1971), 1976

> This medical guide focuses on such adolescent concerns as sex, obesity, smoking, drugs, and suicide.

Hatter Fox, Marilyn Harris (1973), 1976

> Having struggled to survive for seventeen years, Navaho Hatter Fox stabs a reservation doctor, gains his attention, and almost starts a new life.

Hey, White Girl!, Susan Gregory (1970), 1971

> When her family moves from the suburbs, Susan Gregory attends a Chicago ghetto high school in her senior year and becomes much more than another "whitey."

House of Tomorrow, Jean Thompson (1967), 1971

> A pregnant twenty-year-old girl writes in her diary during her stay in a Salvation Army home for unwed mothers.

I Never Promised You a Rose Garden, Joanne Greenberg (1964), 1971

> A sixteen-year-old girl struggles out of the seductive kingdom of her madness and re-enters the real world.

I'm O.K., You're O.K., Thomas A. Harris (1969), 1976

> This popular guide to transactional analysis underscores the elements in each person's psyche and relates them to today's society.

In the Service of Their Country: War Resisters in Prison, Willard Gaylin (1970), 1971

> Six imprisoned war resisters tell their stories as recorded in these compelling case histories by Dr. Gaylin, a psychiatrist.

Journey to Ixtlan, Carlos Casteneda (1974), 1976

> Casteneda breaks away from the use of drugs, is initiated into the world of sorcerers, and learns to "see" rather than merely "look."

Judges, Don Jackson (1974), 1976

> Postulating that the quality of justice reflects the quality of the judges, Jackson portrays examples of some of the good, the bad, and the indifferent.

Learning for Tomorrow: The Role of the Future in Education, Alvin Toffler (1974), 1976

> The future directions of education and curricula are explored in sixteen essays that question current practices.

Long Time Coming, and a Long Time Gone, Richard Farina (1969), 1971

> Richard Farina, a young folk hero who lived only a short time, will be remembered through this posthumous collection of his essays, stories, song lyrics, and poems.

Making of a Counter Culture: Reflections on the Technocratic Society and Its Youthful Opposition, Theodore Roszak (1969), 1971

> The influence of such personalities as Herbert Marcuse, Allen Ginsberg, Timothy Leary, and Paul Goodman are examined together with the leading causes of youthful dissent in the sixties.

Marijuana, Edward R. Bloomquist (1968), 1971

> Through an informal and nonmoralistic approach, and with the use of some excellent cartoons, the author "tells it like it is" about marijuana.

Mr. and Mrs. Bo Jo Jones, Ann Head (1967), 1971

> July and Bo Jo, not yet high school graduates, are already three months into expectant parenthood.

My Lai 4: A Report on the Massacre and Its Aftermath, Seymour M. Hersh (1970), 1971

> A reporter recounts what happens on March 16, 1968, when Charlie Company obliterates the hamlet of My Lai.

Nashville Sound: Bright Lights and Country Music, Paul Hemphill (1970), 1971

> Country-and-western music begins in Nashville.

No More Masks, Florence Howe and Ellen Bass (1973), 1976

> Women poets drop their masks to reveal their female uniqueness.

Nobody Ever Died of Old Age, Sharon R. Curtin (1972), 1976

> Only the elderly themselves can unite and change our society from one that brings them loneliness, discrimination, and insecurity to one that recognizes their rights.

On Being Different: What It Means to Be a Homosexual, Merle Miller (1971), 1976

> With almost fifty years of pretense behind him, this writer admits his homosexuality and analyzes its effect on his life, both publicly and privately.

On Violence, Hannah Arendt (1970), 1971, 1976

> The author explores the reasons why violence is so prevalent in modern society.

One Flew over the Cuckoo's Nest, Ken Kesey (1962), 1976

> An irrepressible rebel leads fellow inmates of a mental hospital in a struggle with tyrannical Head Nurse Ratched.

Open Marriage, a New Life Style for Couples, Nena O'Neill and George O'Neill (1972), 1976

> This manual suggests that monogamous relationships are not fulfilling for all couples; rather, total communication and honesty are the keys to marriage.

Our Bodies, Ourselves, Boston Women's Health Book Collective Staff (1973), 1976

> The total implications of womanhood, from the physical to the psychological, are frankly examined in this personalized and unique guide written by women.

Our Own Worst Enemy, William J. Lederer (1968), 1971

> A longtime student of Asian affairs observes the complexities of the Vietnam War and offers some possible solutions but no panaceas.

Our Time Is Now: Notes from the High School Underground, John Birmingham (1970), 1971

> Uncensored high school students speak of injustices in the schools and of changes needed.

Peace-Love-Thought-God, Peter Max (1970), 1971

> Peter Max illustrates and enlivens the ideas of his spiritual leader.

Peck of Salt: A Year in the Ghetto, John T. Hough Jr. (1970), 1971

> Recollections of a young white VISTA volunteer who served in the beleaguered African American ghettos of Chicago and Detroit.

Poetry of Rock, Richard Goldstein (ed.) (1969), 1971

> Rock and roll lyrics make interesting poetry.

Population Bomb, Paul R. Ehrlich (1968), 1971

> If population growth continues, Ehrlich warns that the world will experience such horrors as widespread famine and multiplying environmental problems.

Price of My Soul, Bernadette Devlin (1969), 1971

> A crusading young Irishwoman and member of Parliament is in and out of jail for her political actions in Ulster.

Psychogeist, L. P. Davies (1967), 1971

> Edward Garvey is reliving a comic book episode involving the character of Angred the Freedman who has grown in Edward's subconscious and now wants a younger, healthier body.

La Raza: The Mexican Americans, Stan Steiner (1970), 1976

> A study of the problems of "The Race," which includes an account of the journey of Cesar Chavez from the boyhood of a migrant farmworker to the role of leader of his people.

Red Sky at Morning, Richard Bradford (1968), 1971

> Joshua Arnold, a wise, wry man-child, must cope with an absent father and a sherry-tippling mother while learning to live in a new town, make friends, and finish growing up.

Right to Privacy, Bill Severn (1973), 1976

> Innocuous requests for personal information by credit unions and public agencies, as well as illegal wiretapping, result in blatant invasion of privacy.

Rock: A Social History of the Music 1945–1972, Mike Jahn (1973), 1976

> This *New York Times* rock critic has observed the scene since the early fifties and answers that perennial question: What does it all mean?

Rock from the Beginning, Nik Cohn (1969), 1971

> The personalities, performing styles, and ethos of pop and rock music are described, from Elvis to the Jefferson Airplane.

Search for the New Land: History as Subjective Experience, Julius Lester (1969), 1971

> Through "found" poems, news clippings, and war chronologies, a sensitive African American militant documents history as he has lived it since the bombing of Hiroshima.

Serpico, Peter Maas (1973), 1976

> Serpico tries to be an honest cop in the New York City Police Department but is thwarted by fellow cops, politicians, and criminals.

Sex before Twenty: New Answers for Youth, Helen F. Southard (1967), 1971

> This book offers practical advice regarding sex and sexuality with emphasis on the total person.

Siddhartha, Hermann Hesse (1951), 1971

> Emerging from a kaleidoscope of experiences and tasted pleasures, Siddhartha transcends to a state of peace and mystic holiness in this strangely simple story.

Silent Sound of Needles, Michael Zwerin (1969), 1971

> Drug addicts undergo rehabilitation at a center in Harlem.

Silent Spring, Rachel Carson (1962), 1971

> Carson raises the first warnings about the destruction of the environment.

Soft Revolution: A Student Handbook for Turning Schools Around, Neil Postman and Charles Weingartner (1971), 1971

> How can schools be changed and humanized without violence?

Soul on Ice, Eldridge Cleaver (1968), 1971

> Through essays and open letters written while in prison, Eldridge Cleaver expresses the inner feelings and drives of the outraged African American man.

Strawberry Statement: Notes of a College Revolutionary, James S. Kunen (1969), 1971

> In diary form, Kunen tells of the 1968 Columbia student uprising and says, "I'm a 19-year-old civilian and I am tired of fighting."

Students without Teachers: The Crisis in the University, Harold Taylor (1969), 1971

> The former president of Sarah Lawrence College writes in detail of the student movement in the United States.

Supership, Noel Mostert (1974), 1976

> *Supership* is a plea for the protection of the ecology of our waterways.

Tell Me That You Love Me, Junie Moon, Marjorie Kellogg (1968), 1971

> Junie Moon, an acid-scarred girl; Warren, a paraplegic; and Arthur, a near spastic, decide to leave the hospital and set up housekeeping together.

Terminal Man, Michael Crichton (1972), 1976

> Even though his own life is threatened, Benson, an epileptic with a computer in his brain, sets out to destroy the ruling machines.

To Be Young, Gifted and Black, Lorraine Hansberry in Her Own Words, Lorraine Hansberry (1969), 1971

> A writer presents a portrait of herself and her view of the human spirit.

To My Brother Who Did a Crime: Former Prisoners Tell Their Stories in Their Own Words, Barbara Habenstreit (ed.) (1973), 1976

> After living most of their lives in a world of drugs, crime, and prison, fourteen young men struggle to "go straight" at Long Island University.

Todd Dossier, Collier Young (1969), 1971

> Financier Hollis Rodd receives a new heart from a young donor whose "accidental" death is questioned by Dr. Charles Everett.

Trial, Tom Hayden (1970), 1971

> Besides giving a personal account of the Chicago Seven trial, Hayden describes the differing politics of the defendants and criticizes the protest movement.

Up Your Banners: A Novel, Donald E. Westlake (1969), 1971

> Oliver, a young white teacher, struggles with a student strike, an African American caucus, militants, an interracial love affair, and his own self-doubts.

Voices of the New Feminism, Mary Lou Thompson (ed.) (1970), 1971

> Twelve women active in the women's liberation movement write on a variety of subjects from "The Liberation of Black Women" to "The Educational Establishment and Women."

Ward 402, Ronald J. Glasser (1973), 1976

> Against the wishes of the father and ignoring the implications of their actions, doctors struggle to keep a young leukemia victim alive.

Weedkiller's Daughter, Harriette Simpson Arnow (1970), 1971

> Caught between her outrageously bigoted father and frightened, empty mother, Susan manages to maintain contacts with people who make her world seem real.

Whole World Is Watching: A Young Man Looks at Youth's Dissent, Mark Gerzon (1969), 1971

> In intelligent, reasoned essays on specifics of the youth scene, a Harvard undergraduate presents his generations's concern for the individual and a more psychologically comfortable, humane world.

Writing on the Wall: 108 American Poems of Protest, Walter Lowenfels (ed.) (1969), 1971

> Martyrdom, inhumanity, war, and death are placed in fierce confrontation with the conscience of the reader.

Your Legal Rights as a Minor, Robert H. Loeb Jr. and John P. Mahoney (1974), 1976

> What are youths' rights in relation to drugs, driving, sex, work, school, parents, buying, and crime?

Zen and the Art of Motorcycle Maintenance, Robert M. Pirsig (1974), 1976

> Pirsig and his son Chris travel across the country by motorcycle, while the reader travels across the metaphysical puzzle that caused Pirsig's mental breakdown.

Outstanding Books for the College Bound

Poetry

Kidnap Poem

Nikki Giovanni

ever been kidnapped

by a poet

if i were a poet

i'd kidnap you

put you in my phrases and meter

you to jones beach

or maybe coney island

or maybe just to my house

lyric you in lilacs

dash you into the beach. . . .

from *Going Over to Your Place:*
Poems for Each Other
by Paul Janeczko

The poetry list is a short one, but note that books of poetry appear in other genres as well, giving a poetic dimension to prose lists.

The books selected here tend to be largely subject anthologies: African American poetry, Japanese poetry, light verse, nature poetry, etc. The books about learning to read, understand, and evaluate poetry will help readers mine the riches of a genre less complicated than it appears—and infinitely rewarding.

Belle of Amherst, William Luce (1976), 1994

Luce's one-act play is based upon the poetry of Emily Dickinson.

Best American Poetry, Donald Hall (1989), 1991

Well-known and beginning poets present their poetry.

Black Poets, Dudley Randall (ed.) (1971), 1988

An anthology encompassing the range of African American poets from singers of slave songs to Nikki Giovanni.

Fifty Modern American and British Poets, 1920–1970, Louis Untermeyer (ed.) (1973), 1988

From Robert Frost to Erica Jong, Untermeyer discusses fifty years of radical change, new tones, new techniques, and a diversity of voices.

Final Harvest: Emily Dickinson's Poems, Emily Dickinson (1962), 1988

In love with words, in love with brevity, Emily Dickinson's poems are like her life—enigmatic, intensely felt, and unforgettable.

Fire in My Hands: A Book of Poems, Gary Soto (1990), 1994

Poems by a Mexican American poet explore the universal themes of growth, family, friendship, and first love.

Going Over to Your Place: Poems for Each Other, Selected by Paul B. Janeczko (1987), 1991

These poems celebrate everyday feelings—from the first kiss to the wonder of a parade.

How to Read and Interpret Poetry, Carole Doreski and William Doreski (1988), 1991

A valuable handbook that helps to evaluate, read, and appreciate poetry in relation to the poet's life.

New Oxford Book of Light Verse, Kingsley Amis (ed.) (1978), 1988

The self-appointed curmudgeon of the British literary world displays editorial quirkiness in his selection of humorous poetry.

One Hundred Poems from the Japanese, Kenneth Rexroth (ed.) (1955), 1988

> A sampler of sensitively translated poems that preserve the beauty and spirit of the original.

Poems for a Small Planet: Contemporary American Nature Poetry, Robert Pack and Jay Parini (eds.) (1993), 1994

> Eighty-three of America's most accomplished poets respond to the plight of nature today.

Poetry of Yevgeny Yevtushenko, Yevgeny Yevtushenko (1981), 1988

> Yevtushenko's poetry is presented in two languages.

Rattle Bag, Seamus Heaney and Ted Hughes (eds.) (1982), 1994

> This compilation of poetry includes poems from the oral tradition.

Sleeping on the Wing: An Anthology of Modern Poetry, with Essays on Reading and Writing, Kenneth Koch and Kate Farrell (1981), 1994

> Essays on the reading and writing of modern poetry complement this contemporary anthology.

Under 35: The New Generation of American Poets, Nicholas Christopher (ed.) (1989), 1991

> Many young poets present poems in a variety of themes and forms.

Vintage Book of Contemporary American Poetry, J. D. McClatchy (ed.) (1990), 1994

> Sixty-five of America's greatest contemporary poets contribute to this comprehensive collection.

PART TWO

The Lists by Year

Outstanding Books for the College Bound

1959–1994

1959 □ FICTION

Austen, Jane	*Pride and Prejudice*
Balzac, Honoré de	*Pere Goriot*
Bellamy, Edward	*Looking Backward: 2000–1887*
Brontë, Charlotte	*Jane Eyre*
Brontö, Emily	*Wuthering Heights*
Buck, Pearl S.	*Good Earth*
Butler, Samuel	*Way of All Flesh*
Cather, Willa	*My Antonia*
Cervantes, Miguel del Saavedra	*Don Quixote de la Mancha*
Collins, Wilkie	*Moonstone*
Conrad, Joseph	*Lord Jim*
Crane, Stephen	*Red Badge of Courage*
Dickens, Charles	*David Copperfield*
Dostoevsky, Fyodor	*Crime and Punishment*
Dreiser, Theodore	*American Tragedy*
Dumas, Alexander	*Count of Monte Cristo*
Eliot, George	*Mill on the Floss*
Fitzgerald, F. Scott	*Great Gatsby*

Fuller, Iola	*Loon Feather*
Galsworthy, John	*Forsyte Saga*
Glasgow, Ellen	*Vein of Iron*
Guareschi, Giovanni	*Little World of Don Camillo*
Hardy, Thomas	*Return of the Native*
Hawthorne, Nathaniel	*Scarlet Letter*
Hemingway, Ernest	*Old Man and the Sea*
Hersey, John	*Single Pebble*
Hudson, W. H.	*Green Mansions*
Hugo, Victor	*Les Miserables*
Kipling, Rudyard	*Kim*
Lewis, Sinclair	*Arrowsmith*
Llewellyn, Richard	*How Green Was My Valley*
Maugham, William Somerset	*Of Human Bondage*
Melville, Herman	*Moby Dick*
Mitchell, Margaret	*Gone with the Wind*
Monsarrat, Nicholas	*Cruel Sea*
Nordhoff, Charles B., and James Norman Hall	*Bounty Trilogy: Comprising the Three Volumes, Mutiny on the Bounty, Men against the Sea, and Pitcairn's Island*
Orwell, George	*Animal Farm*
Page, Elizabeth	*Tree of Liberty*
Paton, Alan	*Cry, the Beloved Country*
Poe, Edgar Allan	*Complete Tales and Poems*
Rawlings, Marjorie Kinnan	*Yearling*
Remarque, Erich Maria	*All Quiet on the Western Front*
Richter, Conrad	*Sea of Grass*
Roberts, Kenneth	*Northwest Passage*
Rolvaag, Ole E.	*Giants in the Earth*
Saroyan, William	*Human Comedy*
Scott, Sir Walter	*Ivanhoe*
Shellabarger, Samuel	*Prince of Foxes*
Sienkiewicz, Henryk	*Quo Vadis*
Steinbeck, John	*Grapes of Wrath*
Stevenson, Robert Louis	*Kidnapped*
Stewart, George	*Storm*
Stone, Irving	*Love Is Eternal*

Thackeray, William Makepeace	*Vanity Fair: A Novel without a Hero*
Tolstoy, Leo	*War and Peace*
Turgenev, Ivan	*Fathers and Sons*
Twain, Mark	*Adventures of Huckleberry Finn*
Undset, Sigrid	*Kristin Lavransdatter*
Wharton, Edith	*Ethan Frome*
Wilder, Thornton	*Bridge of San Luis Rey*

1961 □ BIOGRAPHY

Adams, Henry	*Education of Henry Adams*
Anderson, Marian	*My Lord, What a Morning*
Antin, Mary	*At School in the Promised Land; or, The Story of a Little Immigrant*
Bainton, Roland H.	*Here I Stand: A Life of Martin Luther*
Baruch, Bernard M.	*Baruch, My Own Story*
Bell, Eric T.	*Men of Mathematics*
Boswell, James	*Life of Samuel Johnson*
Bowen, Catherine Drinker	*Yankee from Olympus: Justice Holmes and His Family*
Buck, Pearl S.	*My Several Worlds: A Personal Record*
Castelot, Andre	*Queen of France: A Biography of Marie Antoinette*
Cellini, Benvenuto	*Autobiography of Benvenuto Cellini*
Chute, Marchette	*Shakespeare of London*
Curie, Eve	*Madame Curie; a Biography*
Davis, Burke	*They Called Him Stonewall: A Life of Lt. General T. J. Jackson*
Ferguson, Charles W.	*Naked to Mine Enemies: The Life of Cardinal Wolsey*
Fermi, Laura	*Atoms in the Family: My Life with Enrico Fermi*
Forbes, Esther	*Paul Revere and the World He Lived In*
Frank, Anne	*Anne Frank: The Diary of a Young Girl*
Franklin, Benjamin	*Autobiography*
Gray, Ian	*Peter the Great: Emperor of All Russia*
Guerard, Albert Leon	*Napoleon I*
Hagedorn, Hermann	*Roosevelt Family of Sagamore Hill*

Hart, Moss	*Act One*
Heiser, Victor George	*American Doctor's Odyssey: Adventures in Forty-five Countries*
Jenkins, Elizabeth	*Elizabeth the Great*
Keller, Helen Adams	*Story of My Life*
Kelly, Amy Ruth	*Eleanor of Aquitaine and the Four Kings*
Kennedy, John Fitzgerald	*Profiles in Courage*
Krutch, Joseph Wood	*Henry David Thoreau*
Lamb, Harold	*Suleiman the Magnificent*
Maurois, Andre	*Ariel, the Life of Shelley*
Merton, Thomas	*Seven Storey Mountain*
Morison, Samuel Eliot	*Christopher Columbus, Mariner*
Payne, Robert	*Three Worlds of Albert Schweitzer*
Pepys, Samuel	*Diary of Samuel Pepys*
Plutarch	*Lives*
Roosevelt, Eleanor	*This I Remember*
St. John, Robert	*Ben-Gurion; a Biography*
Steffens, Lincoln	*Autobiography of Lincoln Steffens*
Stone, Irving	*Clarence Darrow for the Defense*
Strachey, Lytton Giles	*Queen Victoria*
Stuart, Jesse	*Thread That Runs So True*
Taylor, Alan J.	*Bismarck: The Man and the Statesman*
Terasaki, Gwen	*Bridge to the Sun*
Tharp, Louise Hall	*Peabody Sisters of Salem*
Thomas, Benjamin P.	*Abraham Lincoln*
Twain, Mark	*Autobiography of Mark Twain*
Van Loon, Hendrik Willem	*R. V. R.: The Life of Rembrandt von Rijn*
Vining, Elizabeth Gray	*Windows for the Crown Prince*
Washington, Booker T.	*Up from Slavery: An Autobiography*
White, William Allen	*Autobiography*
Wong, Jade Snow	*Fifth Chinese Daughter*
Woodham Smith, Cecil	*Florence Nightingale, 1820–1910*

1963 ☐ BIOGRAPHY

Adams, Henry	*Education of Henry Adams*
Anderson, Marian	*My Lord, What a Morning*

Antin, Mary	*At School in the Promised Land; or, The Story of a Little Immigrant*
Bainton, Roland H.	*Here I Stand: A Life of Martin Luther*
Baruch, Bernard M.	*Baruch, My Own Story*
Bell, Eric T.	*Men of Mathematics*
Boswell, James	*Life of Samuel Johnson*
Bowen, Catherine Drinker	*Yankee from Olympus: Justice Holmes and His Family*
Buck, Pearl S.	*My Several Worlds: A Personal Record*
Castelot, Andre	*Queen of France: A Biography of Marie Antoinette*
Cellini, Benvenuto	*Autobiography of Benvenuto Cellini*
Chute, Marchette	*Shakespeare of London*
Cunliffe, Marcus	*George Washington, Man and Monument*
Curie, Eve	*Madame Curie; a Biography*
Davis, Burke	*They Called Him Stonewall: A Life of Lt. General T. J. Jackson*
Ferguson, Charles W.	*Naked to Mine Enemies: The Life of Cardinal Wolsey*
Fermi, Laura	*Atoms in the Family: My Life with Enrico Fermi*
Forbes, Esther	*Paul Revere and the World He Lived In*
Frank, Anne	*Anne Frank: The Diary of a Young Girl*
Franklin, Benjamin	*Autobiography*
Gray, Ian	*Peter the Great: Emperor of All Russia*
Guerard, Albert Leon	*Napoleon I*
Hagedorn, Hermann	*Roosevelt Family of Sagamore Hill*
Hart, Moss	*Act One*
Heiser, Victor George	*American Doctor's Odyssey: Adventures in Forty-five Countries*
Jenkins, Elizabeth	*Elizabeth the Great*
Keller, Helen Adams	*Story of My Life*
Kelly, Amy Ruth	*Eleanor of Aquitaine and the Four Kings*
Kennedy, John Fitzgerald	*Profiles in Courage*
Krutch, Joseph Wood	*Henry David Thoreau*
Lamb, Harold	*Suleiman the Magnificent*
Maurois, Andre	*Ariel, the Life of Shelley*
Merton, Thomas	*Seven Storey Mountain*

Morison, Samuel Eliot	*Christopher Columbus, Mariner*
Payne, Robert	*Three Worlds of Albert Schweitzer*
Pepys, Samuel	*Diary of Samuel Pepys*
Plutarch	*Lives*
Roosevelt, Eleanor	*This I Remember*
St. John, Robert	*Ben-Gurion; a Biography*
Steffens, Lincoln	*Autobiography of Lincoln Steffens*
Stone, Irving	*Clarence Darrow for the Defense*
Strachey, Lytton Giles	*Queen Victoria*
Stuart, Jesse	*Thread That Runs So True*
Taylor, Alan J.	*Bismarck: The Man and the Statesman*
Terasaki, Gwen	*Bridge to the Sun*
Tharp, Louise Hall	*Peabody Sisters of Salem*
Thomas, Benjamin P.	*Abraham Lincoln*
Twain, Mark	*Autobiography of Mark Twain*
Van Loon, Hendrik Willem	*R. V. R.: The Life of Rembrandt von Rijn*
Vining, Elizabeth Gray	*Windows for the Crown Prince*
Washington, Booker T.	*Up from Slavery: An Autobiography*
Wong, Jade Snow	*Fifth Chinese Daughter*

1963 ☐ FICTION

Austen, Jane	*Pride and Prejudice*
Balzac, Honoré de	*Pere Goriot*
Bellamy, Edward	*Looking Backward: 2000–1887*
Brontë, Charlotte	*Jane Eyre*
Brontë, Emily	*Wuthering Heights*
Buck, Pearl S.	*Good Earth*
Butler, Samuel	*Way of All Flesh*
Cather, Willa	*My Antonia*
Cervantes, Miguel del Saavedra	*Don Quixote de la Mancha*
Collins, Wilkie	*Moonstone*
Conrad, Joseph	*Lord Jim*
Crane, Stephen	*Red Badge of Courage*
Dickens, Charles	*David Copperfield*
Dostoevsky, Fyodor	*Crime and Punishment*

Dreiser, Theodore	*American Tragedy*
Dumas, Alexander	*Count of Monte Cristo*
Eliot, George	*Mill on the Floss*
Fitzgerald, F. Scott	*Great Gatsby*
Fuller, Iola	*Loon Feather*
Galsworthy, John	*Forsyte Saga*
Glasgow, Ellen	*Vein of Iron*
Guareschi, Giovanni	*Little World of Don Camillo*
Hardy, Thomas	*Return of the Native*
Hawthorne, Nathaniel	*Scarlet Letter*
Hemingway, Ernest	*Old Man and the Sea*
Hersey, John	*Single Pebble*
Hudson, W. H.	*Green Mansions*
Hugo, Victor	*Les Miserables*
Kipling, Rudyard	*Kim*
Lewis, Sinclair	*Arrowsmith*
Llewellyn, Richard	*How Green Was My Valley*
Maugham, William Somerset	*Of Human Bondage*
Melville, Herman	*Moby Dick*
Mitchell, Margaret	*Gone with the Wind*
Monsarrat, Nicholas	*Cruel Sea*
Nordhoff, Charles B., and James Norman Hall	*Bounty Trilogy: Comprising the Three Volumes, Mutiny on the Bounty, Men against the Sea, and Pitcairn's Island*
Orwell, George	*Animal Farm*
Page, Elizabeth	*Tree of Liberty*
Paton, Alan	*Cry, the Beloved Country*
Poe, Edgar Allan	*Complete Tales and Poems*
Rawlings, Marjorie Kinnan	*Yearling*
Remarque, Erich Maria	*All Quiet on the Western Front*
Richter, Conrad	*Sea of Grass*
Roberts, Kenneth	*Northwest Passage*
Rolvaag, Ole E.	*Giants in the Earth*
Saroyan, William	*Human Comedy*
Scott, Sir Walter	*Ivanhoe*
Shellabarger, Samuel	*Prince of Foxes*
Sienkiewicz, Henryk	*Quo Vadis*

Steinbeck, John	*Grapes of Wrath*
Stevenson, Robert Louis	*Kidnapped*
Stewart, George	*Storm*
Stone, Irving	*Love Is Eternal*
Thackeray, William Makepeace	*Vanity Fair: A Novel without a Hero*
Tolstoy, Leo	*War and Peace*
Turgenev, Ivan	*Fathers and Sons*
Twain, Mark	*Adventures of Huckleberry Finn*
Undset, Sigrid	*Kristin Lavransdatter*
Wharton, Edith	*Ethan Frome*
Wilder, Thornton	*Bridge of San Luis Rey*

1965 ☐ BIOGRAPHY

Adams, Henry	*Education of Henry Adams*
Anderson, Marian	*My Lord, What a Morning*
Antin, Mary	*At School in the Promised Land; or, The Story of a Little Immigrant*
Bainton, Roland H.	*Here I Stand: A Life of Martin Luther*
Baruch, Bernard M.	*Baruch, My Own Story*
Bell, Eric T.	*Men of Mathematics*
Boswell, James	*Life of Samuel Johnson*
Bowen, Catherine Drinker	*Yankee from Olympus: Justice Holmes and His Family*
Buck, Pearl S.	*My Several Worlds: A Personal Record*
Castelot, Andre	*Queen of France: A Biography of Marie Antoinette*
Cellini, Benvenuto	*Autobiography of Benvenuto Cellini*
Chute, Marchette	*Shakespeare of London*
Cunliffe, Marcus	*George Washington, Man and Monument*
Curie, Eve	*Madame Curie; a Biography*
Davis, Burke	*They Called Him Stonewall: A Life of Lt. General T. J. Jackson*
Ferguson, Charles W.	*Naked to Mine Enemies: The Life of Cardinal Wolsey*
Fermi, Laura	*Atoms in the Family: My Life with Enrico Fermi*
Forbes, Esther	*Paul Revere and the World He Lived In*

Frank, Anne	*Anne Frank: The Diary of a Young Girl*
Franklin, Benjamin	*Autobiography*
Gray, Ian	*Peter the Great: Emperor of All Russia*
Guerard, Albert Leon	*Napoleon I*
Hagedorn, Hermann	*Roosevelt Family of Sagamore Hill*
Hart, Moss	*Act One*
Heiser, Victor George	*American Doctor's Odyssey: Adventures in Forty-five Countries*
Jenkins, Elizabeth	*Elizabeth the Great*
Keller, Helen Adams	*Story of My Life*
Kelly, Amy Ruth	*Eleanor of Aquitaine and the Four Kings*
Kennedy, John Fitzgerald	*Profiles in Courage*
Krutch, Joseph Wood	*Henry David Thoreau*
Lamb, Harold	*Suleiman the Magnificent*
Maurois, Andre	*Ariel, the Life of Shelley*
Merton, Thomas	*Seven Storey Mountain*
Morison, Samuel Eliot	*Christopher Columbus, Mariner*
Payne, Robert	*Three Worlds of Albert Schweitzer*
Pepys, Samuel	*Diary of Samuel Pepys*
Plutarch	*Lives*
Roosevelt, Eleanor	*This I Remember*
St. John, Robert	*Ben-Gurion; a Biography*
Steffens, Lincoln	*Autobiography of Lincoln Steffens*
Stone, Irving	*Clarence Darrow for the Defense*
Strachey, Lytton Giles	*Queen Victoria*
Stuart, Jesse	*Thread That Runs So True*
Taylor, Alan J.	*Bismarck: The Man and the Statesman*
Terasaki, Gwen	*Bridge to the Sun*
Tharp, Louise Hall	*Peabody Sisters of Salem*
Thomas, Benjamin P.	*Abraham Lincoln*
Twain, Mark	*Autobiography of Mark Twain*
Van Loon, Hendrik Willem	*R. V. R.: The Life of Rembrandt von Rijn*
Vining, Elizabeth Gray	*Windows for the Crown Prince*
Washington, Booker T.	*Up from Slavery: An Autobiography*
Wong, Jade Snow	*Fifth Chinese Daughter*
Woodham Smith, Cecil	*Florence Nightingale, 1820–1910*

1965 □ FICTION

Austen, Jane	*Pride and Prejudice*
Balzac, Honoré de	*Pere Goriot*
Bellamy, Edward	*Looking Backward: 2000–1887*
Brontë, Charlotte	*Jane Eyre*
Brontë, Emily	*Wuthering Heights*
Buck, Pearl S.	*Good Earth*
Butler, Samuel	*Way of All Flesh*
Cather, Willa	*My Antonia*
Cervantes, Miguel del Saavedra	*Don Quixote de la Mancha*
Collins, Wilkie	*Moonstone*
Conrad, Joseph	*Lord Jim*
Crane, Stephen	*Red Badge of Courage*
Dickens, Charles	*David Copperfield*
Dostoevsky, Fyodor	*Crime and Punishment*
Dreiser, Theodore	*American Tragedy*
Dumas, Alexander	*Count of Monte Cristo*
Eliot, George	*Mill on the Floss*
Fitzgerald, F. Scott	*Great Gatsby*
Fuller, Iola	*Loon Feather*
Galsworthy, John	*Forsyte Saga*
Glasgow, Ellen	*Vein of Iron*
Guareschi, Giovanni	*Little World of Don Camillo*
Hardy, Thomas	*Return of the Native*
Hawthorne, Nathaniel	*Scarlet Letter*
Hemingway, Ernest	*Old Man and the Sea*
Hersey, John	*Single Pebble*
Hudson, W. H.	*Green Mansions*
Hugo, Victor	*Les Miserables*
Kipling, Rudyard	*Kim*
Lewis, Sinclair	*Arrowsmith*
Llewellyn, Richard	*How Green Was My Valley*
Maugham, William Somerset	*Of Human Bondage*
Melville, Herman	*Moby Dick*
Mitchell, Margaret	*Gone with the Wind*
Monsarrat, Nicholas	*Cruel Sea*

Nordhoff, Charles B., and James Norman Hall	*Bounty Trilogy: Comprising the Three Volumes, Mutiny on the Bounty, Men against the Sea, and Pitcairn's Island*
Orwell, George	*Animal Farm*
Page, Elizabeth	*Tree of Liberty*
Paton, Alan	*Cry, the Beloved Country*
Poc, Edgar Allan	*Complete Tales and Poems*
Rawlings, Marjorie Kinnan	*Yearling*
Remarque, Erich Maria	*All Quiet on the Western Front*
Richter, Conrad	*Sea of Grass*
Roberts, Kenneth	*Northwest Passage*
Rolvaag, Ole E.	*Giants in the Earth*
Saroyan, William	*Human Comedy*
Scott, Sir Walter	*Ivanhoe*
Shellabarger, Samuel	*Prince of Foxes*
Sienkiewicz, Henryk	*Quo Vadis*
Steinbeck, John	*Grapes of Wrath*
Stevenson, Robert Louis	*Kidnapped*
Stewart, George	*Storm*
Stone, Irving	*Love Is Eternal*
Thackeray, William Makepeace	*Vanity Fair: A Novel without a Hero*
Tolstoy, Leo	*War and Peace*
Turgenev, Ivan	*Fathers and Sons*
Twain, Mark	*Adventures of Huckleberry Finn*
Undset, Sigrid	*Kristin Lavransdatter*
Wharton, Edith	*Ethan Frome*
Wilder, Thornton	*Bridge of San Luis Rey*

1966 □ THEATER

Anderson, Maxwell	*Winterset*
Beckett, Samuel	*Waiting for Godot*
Besier, Rudolf	*Barretts of Wimpole Street*
Blum, Daniel	*Great Stars of the American Stage: A Pictorial Record*
Blum, Daniel (ed.)	*Theatre World*
Chase, Mary	*Harvey, a Comedy in Three Acts*

Chekhov, Anton	*Cherry Orchard*
Connelly, Marcus Cook	*Green Pastures, a Fable*
Cornell, Katherine	*I Wanted to Be an Actress*
Courtney, Marguerite	*Laurette*
Coward, Noel	*Cavalcade*
Coxe, Louis O., and Robert Chapman	*Billy Budd*
Fowler, Gene	*Good Night, Sweet Prince: The Life and Time of John Barrymore*
Frings, Ketti	*Look Homeward, Angel*
Funke, Lewis (ed.)	*Actors Talk about Acting: Fourteen Interviews with Stars of the Theatre*
Gibson, William	*Miracle Worker; a Play for Television*
Giraudoux, Jean	*Madwoman of Chaillot*
Goetz, Ruth, and August Goetz	*Heiress: A Play*
Gordon, Ruth	*Years Ago*
Green, Stanley	*Rodgers and Hammerstein Story*
Hamilton, Patrick	*Angel Street: A Victorian Thriller in Three Acts*
Hansberry, Lorraine	*Raisin in the Sun*
Harmon, Charlotte	*How to Break into the Theatre*
Hart, Moss	*Act One*
Heggen, Thomas, and Joshua Logan	*Mister Roberts; a Play*
Ibsen, Henrik	*Hedda Gabler*
Kaufman, George S., and Moss Hart	*You Can't Take It with You*
Kesselring, Joseph	*Arsenic and Old Lace*
Lawrence, Jerome, and Robert E. Lee	*Inherit the Wind*
Lindsay, Howard, and Russel Crouse	*Life with Father*
Logan, Joshua	*Wisteria Trees*
Lowe, Frederick	*My Fair Lady*
McCullers, Carson	*Member of the Wedding*
MacLeish, Archibald	*J. B.*
Mantle, Burns	*The Best Plays of . . .*
Marlowe, Christopher	*Doctor Faustus*

Miller, Arthur	*Death of a Salesman*
O'Neill, Eugene	*Ah, Wilderness!*
Patrick, John	*Hasty Heart, a Play in Three Acts*
Prideaux, Tom	*World Theatre in Pictures: From Ancient Times to Modern Broadway*
Rattigan, Terence	*Winslow Boy*
Rodgers, Richard, and Oscar Hammerstein	*Oklahoma!*
Ross, Lillian, and Helen Ross	*Player: A Profile of an Art*
Rostand, Edmond	*Cyrano de Bergerac*
Shakespeare, William	*Hamlet*
Shaw, George Bernard	*Pygmalion*
Sheridan, Richard B.	*School for Scandal*
Sherwood, Robert E.	*Abe Lincoln in Illinois*
Sophocles	*Antigone*
Synge, John Millington	*Playboy of the Western World*
Van Druten, John	*I Remember Mama*
Van Druten, John	*Playwright at Work*
Wilde, Oscar	*Importance of Being Earnest*
Wilder, Thornton	*Our Town*
Williams, Tennessee	*Glass Menagerie*

1967 □ FICTION

Austen, Jane	*Pride and Prejudice*
Balzac, Honoré de	*Pere Goriot*
Brontë, Charlotte	*Jane Eyre*
Brontë, Emily	*Wuthering Heights*
Buck, Pearl S.	*Good Earth*
Butler, Samuel	*Way of All Flesh*
Camus, Albert	*Stranger*
Cather, Willa	*My Antonia*
Cervantes, Miguel del Saavedra	*Don Quixote de la Mancha*
Conrad, Joseph	*Lord Jim*
Crane, Stephen	*Red Badge of Courage*
Dickens, Charles	*David Copperfield*
Dostoevsky, Fyodor	*Crime and Punishment*

Dreiser, Theodore	*American Tragedy*
Eliot, George	*Mill on the Floss*
Faulkner, William	*Sound and the Fury*
Fitzgerald, F. Scott	*Great Gatsby*
Galsworthy, John	*Forsyte Saga*
Golding, William	*Lord of the Flies*
Hardy, Thomas	*Return of the Native*
Hawthorne, Nathaniel	*Scarlet Letter*
Hemingway, Ernest	*Old Man and the Sea*
Hersey, John	*Bell for Adano*
Hudson, W. H.	*Green Mansions*
Hugo, Victor	*Les Miserables*
Huxley, Aldous	*Brave New World*
James, Henry	*Ambassadors*
Knowles, John	*Separate Peace*
Lee, Harper	*To Kill a Mockingbird*
Lewis, Sinclair	*Main Street*
Llewellyn, Richard	*How Green Was My Valley*
Maugham, William Somerset	*Of Human Bondage*
Melville, Herman	*Moby Dick*
Mitchell, Margaret	*Gone with the Wind*
Nordhoff, Charles B., and James Norman Hall	*Bounty Trilogy: Comprising the Three Volumes, Mutiny on the Bounty, Men against the Sea, and Pitcairn's Island*
Orwell, George	*Animal Farm*
Page, Elizabeth	*Tree of Liberty*
Paton, Alan	*Cry, the Beloved Country*
Poe, Edgar Allan	*Complete Tales and Poems*
Remarque, Erich Maria	*All Quiet on the Western Front*
Richter, Conrad	*Sea of Grass*
Roberts, Kenneth	*Northwest Passage*
Rolvaag, Ole E.	*Giants in the Earth*
Salinger, J. D.	*Catcher in the Rye*
Saroyan, William	*Human Comedy*
Scott, Sir Walter	*Ivanhoe*
Sienkiewicz, Henryk	*Quo Vadis*
Steinbeck, John	*Grapes of Wrath*

Stevenson, Robert Louis	*Strange Case of Dr. Jekyll and Mr. Hyde*
Stone, Irving	*Lust for Life: The Novel of Vincent Van Gogh*
Thackeray, William Makepeace	*Vanity Fair: A Novel without a Hero*
Tolstoy, Leo	*War and Peace*
Turgenev, Ivan	*Fathers and Sons*
Twain, Mark	*Adventures of Huckleberry Finn*
Undset, Sigrid	*Kristin Lavransdatter*
Wharton, Edith	*Ethan Frome*
Wilde, Oscar	*Picture of Dorian Gray*
Wilder, Thornton	*Bridge of San Luis Rey*
Wolfe, Thomas	*Look Homeward Angel; a Story of the Buried Life*
Wouk, Herman	*Caine Mutiny*

1968 ☐ BIOGRAPHY

Adams, Henry	*Education of Henry Adams*
Anderson, Marian	*My Lord, What a Morning*
Antin, Mary	*At School in the Promised Land; or, The Story of a Little Immigrant*
Baruch, Bernard M.	*Baruch, My Own Story*
Bell, Eric T.	*Men of Mathematics*
Boswell, James	*Life of Samuel Johnson*
Bowen, Catherine Drinker	*Yankee from Olympus: Justice Holmes and His Family*
Buck, Pearl S.	*My Several Worlds: A Personal Record*
Castelot, Andre	*Queen of France: A Biography of Marie Antoinette*
Cellini, Benvenuto	*Autobiography of Benvenuto Cellini*
Chute, Marchette	*Shakespeare of London*
Cousins, Norman	*Dr. Schweitzer of Lambarene*
Cunliffe, Marcus	*George Washington, Man and Monument*
Curie, Eve	*Madame Curie; a Biography*
Davis, Burke	*They Called Him Stonewall: A Life of Lt. General T. J. Jackson*
De Kruif, Paul Henry	*Microbe Hunters*

Ferguson, Charles W.	*Naked to Mine Enemies: The Life of Cardinal Wolsey*
Fermi, Laura	*Atoms in the Family: My Life with Enrico Fermi*
Forbes, Esther	*Paul Revere and the World He Lived In*
Frank, Anne	*Anne Frank: The Diary of a Young Girl*
Franklin, Benjamin	*Autobiography*
Gray, Ian	*Peter the Great: Emperor of All Russia*
Guerard, Albert Leon	*Napoleon I*
Hagedorn, Hermann	*Roosevelt Family of Sagamore Hill*
Hart, Moss	*Act One*
Heiser, Victor George	*American Doctor's Odyssey: Adventures in Forty-five Countries*
Jenkins, Elizabeth	*Elizabeth the Great*
Keller, Helen Adams	*Story of My Life*
Kelly, Amy Ruth	*Eleanor of Aquitaine and the Four Kings*
Kennedy, John Fitzgerald	*Profiles in Courage*
Krutch, Joseph Wood	*Henry David Thoreau*
Lamb, Harold	*Hannibal: One Man against Rome*
Maurois, Andre	*Ariel, the Life of Shelley*
Merton, Thomas	*Seven Storey Mountain*
Morison, Samuel Eliot	*Christopher Columbus, Mariner*
Pepys, Samuel	*Diary of Samuel Pepys*
Plutarch	*Lives*
Roosevelt, Eleanor	*This I Remember*
Sandburg, Carl	*Abraham Lincoln: The Prairie Years and the War Years*
Sandburg, Carl	*Always the Young Strangers*
St. John, Robert	*Ben-Gurion; a Biography*
Steffens, Lincoln	*Autobiography of Lincoln Steffens*
Stone, Irving	*Clarence Darrow for the Defense*
Strachey, Lytton Giles	*Queen Victoria*
Stuart, Jesse	*Thread That Runs So True*
Taylor, Alan J.	*Bismarck: The Man and the Statesman*
Tharp, Louise Hall	*Peabody Sisters of Salem*
Twain, Mark	*Autobiography of Mark Twain*
Van Loon, Hendrik Willem	*R. V. R.: The Life of Rembrandt von Rijn*

Vining, Elizabeth Gray	*Windows for the Crown Prince*
Washington, Booker T.	*Up from Slavery: An Autobiography*
Winwar, Frances	*Haunted Palace: A Life of Edgar Allan Poe*
Wong, Jade Snow	*Fifth Chinese Daughter*
Woolf, Virginia	*Flush: A Biography*
Yevtushenko, Yevgeny	*Precocious Autobiography*

1968 □ THEATER

Anderson, Maxwell	*Winterset*
Baldwin, James	*Amen Corner*
Beckett, Samuel	*Waiting for Godot*
Blum, Daniel	*Great Stars of the American Stage: A Pictorial Record*
Blum, Daniel (ed.)	*Theatre World*
Brecht, Bertolt	*Mother Courage and Her Children: A Chronicle of the Thirty Years War*
Brustein, Robert	*Third Theatre*
Chekhov, Anton	*Cherry Orchard*
Courtney, Marguerite	*Laurette*
Fowler, Gene	*Good Night, Sweet Prince: The Life and Time of John Barrymore*
Funke, Lewis (ed.)	*Actors Talk about Acting: Fourteen Interviews with Stars of the Theatre*
Gibson, William	*Miracle Worker; a Play for Television*
Giraudoux, Jean	*Madwoman of Chaillot*
Goetz, Ruth, and August Goetz	*Heiress: A Play*
Hansberry, Lorraine	*Raisin in the Sun*
Heggen, Thomas, and Joshua Logan	*Mister Roberts; a Play*
Hellman, Lillian	*Little Foxes*
Ibsen, Henrik	*Hedda Gabler*
Kaufman, George S., and Moss Hart	*You Can't Take It with You*
Lawrence, Jerome, and Robert E. Lee	*Inherit the Wind*
Leigh, Mitch	*Man of La Mancha*

Lindsay, Howard, and Russel Crouse	*Life with Father*
Lorca, Federico Garcia	*Blood Wedding*
McCullers, Carson	*Member of the Wedding*
MacLeish, Archibald	*J. B.*
Mantle, Burns	*The Best Plays of . . .*
Marlowe, Christopher	*Doctor Faustus*
Miller, Arthur	*Death of a Salesman*
O'Neill, Eugene	*Long Day's Journey into Night*
Prideaux, Tom	*World Theatre in Pictures: From Ancient Times to Modern Broadway*
Rattigan, Terence	*Winslow Boy*
Rodgers, Richard, and Oscar Hammerstein	*Oklahoma!*
Ross, Lillian, and Helen Ross	*Player: A Profile of an Art*
Sartre, Jean Paul	*No Exit*
Shakespeare, William	*Hamlet*
Shaw, George Bernard	*Pygmalion*
Sheridan, Richard B.	*School for Scandal*
Sherwood, Robert E.	*Abe Lincoln in Illinois*
Sophocles	*Antigone*
Stein, Joseph	*Fiddler on the Roof*
Synge, John Millington	*Playboy of the Western World*
Webster, Margaret	*Same Only Different: Five Generations of a Great Theatre Family*
Wilde, Oscar	*Importance of Being Earnest*
Wilder, Thornton	*Our Town*
Williams, Tennessee	*Glass Menagerie*

1971 ☐ BIOGRAPHY

Bainton, Roland H.	*Here I Stand: A Life of Martin Luther*
Baker, Carlos	*Ernest Hemingway: A Life Story*
Bennett, Lerone	*What Manner of Man: Biography of Martin Luther King, Jr.*
Boswell, James	*Life of Samuel Johnson*
Bowen, Catherine Drinker	*Yankee from Olympus: Justice Holmes and His Family*

Brown, Claude	*Manchild in the Promised Land*
Cellini, Benvenuto	*Autobiography of Benvenuto Cellini*
Chute, Marchette	*Geoffrey Chaucer of England*
Clarke, John Henrik	*Malcolm X: The Man and His Times*
Curie, Eve	*Madame Curie; a Biography*
De Beer, Sir Gavin	*Hannibal: Challenging Rome's Supremacy*
De Kruif, Paul Henry	*Microbe Hunters*
Ferguson, Charles W.	*Naked to Mine Enemies: The Life of Cardinal Wolsey*
Fermi, Laura	*Atoms in the Family: My Life with Enrico Fermi*
Forbes, Esther	*Paul Revere and the World He Lived In*
Frank, Anne	*Anne Frank: The Diary of a Young Girl*
Franklin, Benjamin	*Autobiography*
Fraser, Antonia	*Mary, Queen of Scots*
Gray, Ian	*Peter the Great: Emperor of All Russia*
Guerard, Albert Leon	*Napoleon I*
Hagedorn, Hermann	*Roosevelt Family of Sagamore Hill*
Hansberry, Lorraine	*To Be Young, Gifted and Black, Lorraine Hansberry in Her Own Words*
Hart, Moss	*Act One*
Jenkins, Elizabeth	*Elizabeth the Great*
Keller, Helen Adams	*Story of My Life*
Kelly, Amy Ruth	*Eleanor of Aquitaine and the Four Kings*
Kennedy, John Fitzgerald	*Profiles in Courage*
Martin, Ralph G.	*Jennie: The Life of Lady Randolph Churchill, Vol. I: The Romantic Years 1854–1895*
Maurois, Andre	*Ariel, the Life of Shelley*
Merton, Thomas	*Seven Storey Mountain*
Moody, Anne	*Coming of Age in Mississippi: An Autobiography*
Morison, Samuel Eliot	*Christopher Columbus, Mariner*
Parks, Gordon	*Choice of Weapons*
Pepys, Samuel	*Diary of Samuel Pepys*
Plutarch	*Lives*
Rowse, Alfred Leslie	*William Shakespeare: A Biography*

Sandburg, Carl	*Abraham Lincoln: The Prairie Years and the War Years*
Sandburg, Carl	*Always the Young Strangers*
Skinner, Cornelia	*Madame Sarah*
St. John, Robert	*Ben-Gurion; a Biography*
Steffens, Lincoln	*Autobiography of Lincoln Steffens*
Stone, Irving	*Clarence Darrow for the Defense*
Strachey, Lytton Giles	*Queen Victoria*
Stuart, Jesse	*Thread That Runs So True*
Taylor, Alan J.	*Bismarck: The Man and the Statesman*
Tharp, Louise Hall	*Peabody Sisters of Salem*
Twain, Mark	*Autobiography of Mark Twain*
Washington, Booker T.	*Up from Slavery: An Autobiography*
Watson, James D., and Guntor S. Stent (ed.)	*Double Helix: A Personal Account of the Discovery of the Structure of DNA*
Winwar, Frances	*Haunted Palace: A Life of Edgar Allan Poe*
Yevtushenko, Yevgeny	*Precocious Autobiography*

1971 □ FICTION

Agee, James	*Death in the Family*
Austen, Jane	*Pride and Prejudice*
Bellow, Saul	*Adventures of Augie March*
Brontë, Charlotte	*Jane Eyre*
Brontë, Emily	*Wuthering Heights*
Buck, Pearl S.	*Good Earth*
Camus, Albert	*Plague*
Cather, Willa	*My Antonia*
Cervantes, Miguel del Saavedra	*Don Quixote de la Mancha*
Collins, Wilkie	*Moonstone*
Conrad, Joseph	*Lord Jim*
Crane, Stephen	*Red Badge of Courage*
Dickens, Charles	*Bleak House*
Dostoevsky, Fyodor	*Crime and Punishment*
Ellison, Ralph	*Invisible Man*
Faulkner, William	*Sound and the Fury*

Fitzgerald, F. Scott	*Great Gatsby*
Flaubert, Gustave	*Madame Bovary*
Forster, E. M.	*Passage to India*
Golding, William	*Lord of the Flies*
Grass, Günter	*Tin Drum*
Hemingway, Ernest	*For Whom the Bell Tolls*
Hugo, Victor	*Les Miserables*
Huxley, Aldous	*Brave New World*
James, Henry	*Turn of the Screw*
Kafka, Franz	*Trial*
Kazantzakis, Nikos	*Zorba the Greek*
Keyes, Daniel	*Flowers for Algernon*
Knowles, John	*Separate Peace*
Lawrence, David Herbert	*Sons and Lovers*
Lee, Harper	*To Kill a Mockingbird*
Lewis, Sinclair	*Main Street*
Malamud, Bernard	*Fixer*
Malraux, André	*Man's Fate*
Mann, Thomas	*Magic Mountain*
Markandaya, Kamala	*Nectar in a Sieve*
Maugham, William Somerset	*Of Human Bondage*
Melville, Herman	*Moby Dick*
Mishima, Yukio	*Sound of Waves*
Mitchell, Margaret	*Gone with the Wind*
Orwell, George	*1984*
Paton, Alan	*Cry, the Beloved Country*
Remarque, Erich Maria	*All Quiet on the Western Front*
Rolvaag, Ole E.	*Giants in the Earth*
Saint-Exupery, Antoine de	*Little Prince*
Salinger, J. D.	*Catcher in the Rye*
Solzhenitsyn, Alexander	*One Day in the Life of Ivan Denisovich*
Steinbeck, John	*Grapes of Wrath*
Tolkien, J. R. R.	*Lord of the Rings*
Tolstoy, Leo	*Anna Karenina*
Twain, Mark	*Adventures of Huckleberry Finn*
Undset, Sigrid	*Kristin Lavransdatter*
Vonnegut, Kurt	*Cat's Cradle*

Wharton, Edith	*Ethan Frome*
Wilde, Oscar	*Picture of Dorian Gray*
Wilder, Thornton	*Bridge of San Luis Rey*
Wolfe, Thomas	*Look Homeward Angel; a Story of the Buried Life*
Wright, Richard	*Native Son*

1971 □ NONFICTION

Bernstein, Leonard	*Joy of Music*
Brinton, Crane	*Ideas and Men: The Story of Western Thought*
Canaday, John	*Mainstreams of Modern Art*
Carson, Rachel	*Sea around Us*
Ceram, C. W.	*Gods, Graves, and Scholars: The Story of Archaeology*
Ciardi, John	*How Does a Poem Mean*
Clark, Kenneth	*Civilisation: A Personal View*
Dantzig, Tobias	*Number: The Language of Science*
Ebenstein, William, and Edwin Fogelman	*Today's Isms: Communism, Fascism, Capitalism, Socialism*
Eisely, Loren	*Darwin's Century: Evolution and the Men Who Discovered It*
Feldman, Edmund Burke	*Art as Image and Idea*
Galbraith, John Kenneth	*New Industrial State*
Gamow, George	*One Two Three—Infinity: Facts and Speculations of Science*
Giedion, Siegfried	*Space, Time and Architecture*
Hamilton, Edith	*Mythology*
Harrington, Michael	*Other America: Poverty in the United States*
Heilbroner, Robert L.	*Worldly Philosophers: The Lives, Times and Ideas of the Great Economic Thinkers*
Hofstadter, Richard	*American Political Tradition and the Men Who Made It*
Hosken, Fran P.	*Language of Cities*
Inkeles, Alex	*What Is Sociology: An Introduction to the Discipline and Profession*

Janson, H. W., and Joseph Kerman	*History of Art and Music*
Kaplan, Abraham	*New World of Philosophy*
Lidz, Theodore	*Person: His and Her Development throughout the Life Cycle*
Lorenz, Konrad	*On Aggression*
McNeil, William	*World History*
Mansbridge, John	*Graphic History of Architecture*
Myrdal, Gunnar	*American Dilemma: The Negro Problem and Modern Democracy*
Nevins, Allan	*Gateway to History*
Randall, John H., and Justus Buchler	*Philosophy: An Introduction*
Russell, Bertrand	*History of Western Philosophy*
Snow, C. P.	*Two Cultures*
Steiner, Stan	*La Raza: The Mexican Americans*
Taylor, Joshua C.	*Learning to Look: A Handbook for the Visual Arts*
Thomson, Robert	*Pelican History of Psychology*
Tocqueville, Alexis de	*Democracy in America*
Voss, Carl	*In Search of Meaning, Living Religions of the World*
Wellek, Rene, and Austin Warren	*Theory of Literature*

1971 □ NOW/CURRENT

Arendt, Hannah	*On Violence*
Arnow, Harriette Simpson	*Weedkiller's Daughter*
Baez, Joan	*Daybreak*
Birmingham, John	*Our Time Is Now: Notes from the High School Underground*
Bloomquist, Edward R.	*Marijuana*
Bradford, Richard	*Red Sky at Morning*
Carson, Rachel	*Silent Spring*
Cleaver, Eldridge	*Soul on Ice*
Cohn, Nik	*Rock from the Beginning*
Crichton, Michael	*Andromeda Strain*

Davies, L. P.   *Psychogeist*
De Bell, Garrett (comp.)   *Environmental Handbook*
Deloria Jr., Vine   *Custer Died for Your Sins: An Indian
                                      Manifesto*
Devlin, Bernadette   *Price of My Soul*
Ehrlich, Paul R.   *Population Bomb*
Farina, Richard   *Long Time Coming, and a Long Time
                                      Gone*
Gaylin, Willard   *In the Service of Their Country: War
                                      Resisters in Prison*
Gerzon, Mark   *Whole World Is Watching: A Young Man
                                      Looks at Youth's Dissent*
Goldstein, Richard (ed.)   *Poetry of Rock*
Greenberg, Joanne   *I Never Promised You a Rose Garden*
Gregory, Susan   *Hey, White Girl!*
Hansberry, Lorraine   *To Be Young, Gifted and Black, Lorraine
                                      Hansberry in Her Own Words*
Hayden, Tom   *Trial*
Head, Ann   *Mr. and Mrs. Bo Jo Jones*
Heller, Joseph   *Catch-22*
Hemphill, Paul   *Nashville Sound: Bright Lights and Coun-
                                      try Music*
Hersh, Seymour M.   *My Lai 4: A Report on the Massacre and
                                      Its Aftermath*
Hesse, Hermann   *Siddhartha*
Hopkins, Jerry   *Festival! The Book of American Musical
                                      Celebrations*
Hough Jr., John T.   *Peck of Salt: A Year in the Ghetto*
Kellogg, Marjorie   *Tell Me That You Love Me, Junie Moon*
Kunen, James S.   *Strawberry Statement: Notes of a College
                                      Revolutionary*
Lederer, William J.   *Our Own Worst Enemy*
Lester, Julius   *Search for the New Land: History as Sub-
                                      jective Experience*
Louria, Donald B.   *Drug Scene*
Lowenfels, Walter (ed.)   *Writing on the Wall: 108 American Poems
                                      of Protest*
Malamud, Bernard   *The Fixer*
Max, Peter   *Peace-Love-Thought-God*

Mead, Margaret — *Culture and Commitment: The New Relationships between the Generations in the 1970's*

Owens, Jesse — *Blackthink: My Life as a Black Man and White Man*

Postman, Neil, and Charles Weingartner — *Soft Revolution: A Student Handbook for Turning Schools Around*

Roszak, Theodore — *Making of a Counter Culture: Reflections on the Technocratic Society and Its Youthful Opposition*

Southard, Helen F. — *Sex before Twenty: New Answers for Youth*

Swarthout, Glendon — *Bless the Beasts and Children*

Taylor, Gordon Rattray — *Biological Time Bomb*

Taylor, Harold — *Students without Teachers: The Crisis in the University*

Thompson, Jean — *House of Tomorrow*

Thompson, Mary Lou (ed.) — *Voices of the New Feminism*

Toffler, Alvin — *Future Shock*

Travers, Milton — *Each Other's Victims*

Westlake, Donald E. — *Up Your Banners: A Novel*

X, Malcolm — *Autobiography of Malcolm X*

Young, Collier — *Todd Dossier*

Zwerin, Michael — *Silent Sound of Needles*

1971 ☐ THEATER

Albee, Edward — *Zoo Story*

Anderson, Maxwell — *Winterset*

Anonymous — *Everyman*

Aristophanes — *Lysistrata*

Beckett, Samuel — *Waiting for Godot*

Behan, Brendan — *Hostage*

Bentley, Eric — *Theater of Commitment*

Bentley, Eric — *What Is Theater: A Query in Chronicle Form*

Bolt, Robert — *Man for All Seasons*

Brecht, Bertolt — *Mother Courage and Her Children: A Chronicle of the Thirty Years War*

Brustein, Robert	*Theater of Revolt: An Approach to the Modern Drama*
Chekhov, Anton	*Cherry Orchard*
Cheney, Sheldon	*Theatre: Three Thousand Years of Drama, Acting and Stagecraft*
Congreve, William	*Way of the World*
Eliot, T. S.	*Murder in the Cathedral*
Esslin, Martin	*Reflections: Essays on Modern Theater*
Esslin, Martin	*Theater of the Absurd*
Fergusson, Francis	*Idea of a Theatre: A Study of Ten Plays, the Art of Drama in Changing Perspective*
Gassner, John	*Masters of the Drama*
Gibson, William	*Miracle Worker; a Play for Television*
Giraudoux, Jean	*Madwoman of Chaillot*
Goldman, James	*Lion in Winter*
Grotowski, Jerzy	*Towards a Poor Theater*
Hansberry, Lorraine	*Raisin in the Sun*
Harbage, Alfred	*William Shakespeare: A Reader's Guide*
Hellman, Lillian	*Little Foxes*
Hochhuth, Rolf	*Deputy*
Ibsen, Henrik	*Enemy of the People*
Ionesco, Eugene	*Rhinoceros*
Kaufman, George S., and Moss Hart	*You Can't Take It with You*
Kerr, Walter	*Theater in Spite of Itself*
Kostelanetz, Richard	*Theater of Mixed Means*
Lawrence, Jerome, and Robert E. Lee	*Inherit the Wind*
Lewin, John	*House of Atreus: Adapted from the Oresteia*
Lorca, Federico Garcia	*Blood Wedding*
Luke, Peter	*Hadrian VII, a Play*
McCullers, Carson	*Member of the Wedding*
MacDermot, Galt	*Hair*
MacLeish, Archibald	*J.B.*
Marlowe, Christopher	*Doctor Faustus*
Miller, Arthur	*Crucible*

Molière, Jean	*Miser*
Nicoll, Allardyce	*Development of the Theater: A Study of Theatrical Art from the Beginnings to Present Day*
O'Casey, Sean	*Juno and the Paycock*
O'Neill, Eugene	*Long Day's Journey into Night*
Osborne, John	*Look Back in Anger, a Play in Three Acts*
Pinter, Harold	*Birthday Party*
Pirandello, Luigi	*Six Characters in Search of an Author*
Racine, Jean Baptiste	*Phaedra*
Rattigan, Terence	*Winslow Boy*
Rodgers, Richard, and Oscar Hammerstein	*Oklahoma!*
Rostand, Edmond	*Cyrano de Bergerac*
Sackler, Howard	*Great White Hope: A Play*
Sartre, Jean Paul	*No Exit*
Shakespeare, William	*Midsummer Night's Dream*
Shakespeare, William	*Othello*
Shaw, George Bernard	*Saint Joan*
Sheridan, Richard B.	*School for Scandal*
Simon, Neil	*Odd Couple*
Sophocles	*Oedipus the King*
Stein, Joseph	*Fiddler on the Roof*
Stoppard, Tom	*Rosencrantz and Guildenstern Are Dead*
Strindberg, August	*Father*
Synge, John Millington	*Playboy of the Western World*
Taylor, John Russell	*Angry Theater: New British Drama*
Wilde, Oscar	*Importance of Being Earnest*
Wilder, Thornton	*Our Town*
Williams, Tennessee	*Glass Menagerie*

1976 □ BIOGRAPHY

Bainton, Roland H.	*Here I Stand: A Life of Martin Luther*
Bourke-White, Margaret	*Portrait of Myself*
Bowen, Catherine Drinker	*Most Dangerous Man in America: Scenes from the Life of Benjamin Franklin*

Brodie, Fawn McKay   *Thomas Jefferson: An Intimate History*

Brown, Claude   *Manchild in the Promised Land*

Bullock, Alan Louis   *Hitler, a Study in Tyranny*

Burgess, Alan   *Daylight Must Come: The Story of a Courageous Woman Doctor in the Congo*

Carrighar, Sally   *Home to the Wilderness*

Chandler, David   *Napoleon*

Clark, Ronald W.   *Einstein: The Life and Times*

Curie, Eve   *Madame Curie; a Biography*

Douglas, William O.   *Go East, Young Man: The Early Years; the Autobiography of William O. Douglas*

Halberstam, David   *Ho*

Hibbard, Howard   *Michelangelo*

Hotchner, A. E.   *Papa Hemingway: A Personal Memoir*

Jenkins, Elizabeth   *Elizabeth the Great*

Keller, Helen Adams   *Story of My Life*

Kennedy, John Fitzgerald   *Profiles in Courage*

Lash, Joseph P.   *Eleanor and Franklin: The Story of Their Relationship, Based on Eleanor Roosevelt's Private Papers*

Lund, Doris   *Eric*

McClellan, David   *Karl Marx: His Life and Thought*

Mann, Peggy   *Golda: The Life of Israel's Prime Minister*

Massie, Robert K.   *Nicholas and Alexandra*

Mead, Margaret   *Blackberry Winter: My Earlier Years*

Merriam, Eve (ed.)   *Growing Up Female in America—Ten Lives*

Milford, Nancy   *Zelda: A Biography*

Miller, Merle   *Plain Speaking: An Oral Biography of Harry S. Truman*

Pepys, Samuel   *Diary of Samuel Pepys*

Sandburg, Carl   *Abraham Lincoln: The Prairie Years and the War Years*

Sanders, Marion K.   *Dorothy Thompson: A Legend in Her Time*

Stone, Irving   *Clarence Darrow for the Defense*

Tomalin, Claire   *Life and Death of Mary Wollenstonecraft*

Twombly, Robert C.	*Frank Lloyd Wright: An Interpretive Biography*
Wilson, Dorothy Clarke	*Bright Eyes: The Story of Susette La Flesche, an Omaha Indian*
Wolfe, Bertram David	*Three Who Made a Revolution: A Biographical History*
Wright, Richard	*Black Boy: A Record of Childhood and Youth*
Wyeth, N. C.	*N. C. Wyeth: The Collected Paintings, Illustrations, and Murals*
X, Malcolm	*Autobiography of Malcolm X*
Zassenhaus, Hiltgunt	*Walls: Resisting the Third Reich—One Woman's Story*

1976 □ FICTION

Austen, Jane	*Pride and Prejudice*
Baldwin, James	*Go Tell It on the Mountain*
Camus, Albert	*Stranger*
Cather, Willa	*My Antonia*
Cervantes, Miguel del Saavedra	*Don Quixote de la Mancha*
Conrad, Joseph	*Great Short Works of Joseph Conrad*
Crane, Stephen	*Red Badge of Courage*
Dickens, Charles	*Great Expectations*
Dostoevsky, Fyodor	*Crime and Punishment*
Ellison, Ralph	*Invisible Man*
Faulkner, William	*Sound and the Fury*
Fitzgerald, F. Scott	*Great Gatsby*
Gardner, John	*Grendel*
Golding, William	*Lord of the Flies*
Greenberg, Joanne	*I Never Promised You a Rose Garden*
Hardy, Thomas	*Return of the Native*
Hawthorne, Nathaniel	*Scarlet Letter*
Heller, Joseph	*Catch-22*
Hemingway, Ernest	*For Whom the Bell Tolls*
Hesse, Hermann	*Siddhartha*
Huxley, Aldous	*Brave New World*
Joyce, James	*Portrait of the Artist as a Young Man*

Kafka, Franz	*Metamorphosis*
Knowles, John	*Separate Peace*
Kosinski, Jerzy N.	*Painted Bird*
Lawrence, David Herbert	*Sons and Lovers*
Le Guin, Ursula K.	*Left Hand of Darkness*
Lewis, Sinclair	*Main Street*
Malamud, Bernard	*Fixer*
Mann, Thomas	*Death in Venice*
Maugham, William Somerset	*Of Human Bondage*
Melville, Herman	*Moby Dick*
Paton, Alan	*Cry, the Beloved Country*
Poe, Edgar Allan	*Fall of the House of Usher and Other Tales*
Remarque, Erich Maria	*All Quiet on the Western Front*
Salinger, J. D.	*Catcher in the Rye*
Solzhenitsyn, Alexander	*Gulag Archipelago 1918–1956: An Experiment in Literary Investigation*
Solzhenitsyn, Alexander	*One Day in the Life of Ivan Denisovich*
Steinbeck, John	*Grapes of Wrath*
Swift, Jonathan	*Gulliver's Travels*
Tolkien, J. R. R.	*Lord of the Rings*
Tolstoy, Leo	*War and Peace*
Twain, Mark	*Adventures of Huckleberry Finn*
Vonnegut, Kurt	*Slaughterhouse Five; or, The Children's Crusade*
Wolfe, Thomas	*Look Homeward Angel; a Story of the Buried Life*
Wright, Richard	*Native Son*

1976 □ NONFICTION

Agee, James, and Walker Evans	*Let Us Now Praise Famous Men*
Ballou, Robert O. (ed.)	*Portable World Bible*
Benedict, Ruth Fulton	*Patterns of Culture*
Bennett, Lerone	*Before the Mayflower: A History of the Negro in America, 1619–1964*

Bronowski, Jacob	*Ascent of Man*
Brown, Dee	*Bury My Heart at Wounded Knee: An Indian History of the American West*
Carson, Rachel	*Silent Spring*
Ceram, C. W.	*Gods, Graves, and Scholars: The Story of Archaeology*
Ciardi, John	*How Does a Poem Mean*
Cooke, Alistair	*Alistair Cooke's America*
Copland, Aaron	*What to Listen For in Music*
Durant, William J.	*Story of Philosophy*
Ebenstein, William, and Edwin Fogelman	*Today's Isms. Communism, Fascism, Capitalism, Socialism*
Eisely, Loren	*Darwin's Century: Evolution and the Men Who Discovered It*
Friedan, Betty	*Feminine Mystique*
Fuller, R. Buckminster	*Operating Manual for Spaceship Earth*
Hamilton, Edith	*Mythology*
Heilbroner, Robert L.	*Worldly Philosophers: The Lives, Times and Ideas of the Great Economic Thinkers*
Hoffer, Eric	*True Believer: Thoughts on the Nature of Mass Movements*
Homer	*Odyssey of Homer: A Modern Translation*
Jacobs, Jane	*Death and Life of Great American Cities*
Jungk, Robert	*Brighter than a Thousand Suns: A Personal History of the Atomic Scientists*
Kaplan, Abraham	*New World of Philosophy*
Kline, Morris	*Mathematics in Western Culture*
Kuh, Katherine	*Break-Up: The Core of Modern Art*
Lorenz, Konrad	*On Aggression*
McLuhan, Marshall	*Understanding Media: The Extensions of Man*
Magnuson, Warren, and Jean Carper	*Dark Side of the Marketplace: The Plight of the American Consumer*
Neill, Alexander Sutherland	*Summerhill: A Radical Approach to Child Rearing*
Redman, Eric	*Dance of Legislation*

Roszak, Theodore	*Making of a Counter Culture: Reflections on the Technocratic Society and Its Youthful Opposition*
Schlesinger, M. Arthur	*Imperial Presidency*
Taylor, Joshua C.	*Learning to Look: A Handbook for the Visual Arts*
Terkel, Studs	*Working: People Talk about What They Do All Day and How They Feel about What They Do*
Thomas, Lewis	*Lives of a Cell: Notes of a Biology Watcher*
Thoreau, Henry David	*Walden and Civil Disobedience*
Tocqueville, Alexis de	*Democracy in America*
Toffler, Alvin	*Future Shock*
Watson, James D., and Guntor S. Stent (ed.)	*Double Helix: A Personal Account of the Discovery of the Structure of DNA*
Woodward, Comer Vann	*Strange Career of Jim Crow*

1976 □ NOW/CURRENT

Arendt, Hannah	*On Violence*
Bernstein, Carl, and Bob Woodward	*All the President's Men*
Boston Women's Health Book Collective Staff	*Our Bodies, Ourselves*
Cameron, John	*Astrologer*
Casteneda, Carlos	*Journey to Ixtlan*
Collins, Michael	*Carrying the Fire: An Astronaut's Journeys*
Commoner, Barry	*Closing Circle*
Cormier, Robert	*Chocolate War*
Crichton, Michael	*Terminal Man*
Curtin, Sharon R.	*Nobody Ever Died of Old Age*
Deloria Jr., Vine	*Custer Died for Your Sins: An Indian Manifesto*
Fast, Julius	*Body Language*
Friedman, Myra	*Buried Alive: The Biography of Janis Joplin*
Gersch, Marvin J., and Iris F. Litt	*Handbook of Adolescence*

Glasser, Ronald J.	*Ward 402*
Grier, William H., and Price M. Cobbs	*Black Rage*
Habenstreit, Barbara (ed.)	*To My Brother Who Did a Crime: Former Prisoners Tell Their Stories in Their Own Words*
Harris, Marilyn	*Hatter Fox*
Harris, Thomas A.	*I'm O.K., You're O.K.*
Holt, John	*Escape from Childhood*
Howe, Florence, and Ellen Bass	*No More Masks*
Jackson, Don	*Judges*
Jahn, Mike	*Rock: A Social History of the Music 1945–1972*
Janeway, Elizabeth	*Between Myth and Morning: Women Awakening*
Kesey, Ken	*One Flew over the Cuckoo's Nest*
Kusche, Larry	*Bermuda Triangle Mystery Solved*
Langone, John	*Death Is a Noun: A View of the End of Life*
Loeb Jr., Robert H., and John P. Mahoney	*Your Legal Rights as a Minor*
Maas, Peter	*Serpico*
Mead, Margaret	*Culture and Commitment: The New Relationships between the Generations in the 1970's*
Miller, Merle	*On Being Different: What It Means to Be a Homosexual*
Mostert, Noel	*Supership*
O'Neill, Nena, and George O'Neill	*Open Marriage, a New Life Style for Couples*
Pines, Maya	*Brain Changers: Scientists and the New Mind Control*
Pirsig, Robert M.	*Zen and the Art of Motorcycle Maintenance*
Plath, Sylvia	*Bell Jar*
Read, Piers Paul	*Alive: The Story of the Andes Survivors*
Severn, Bill	*Right to Privacy*
Steiner, Stan	*La Raza: The Mexican Americans*
Tidyman, Ernest	*Dummy*

Toffler, Alvin	*Learning for Tomorrow: The Role of the Future in Education*
Verrett, Jacqueline, and Jean Carper	*Eating May Be Hazardous to Your Health, How Your Government Fails to Protect You from the Dangers in Your Food*
Wigginton, Eliot (ed.)	*Foxfire Book*
Yette, Samuel F.	*Choice: The Issue of Black Survival in America*

1976 ☐ THEATER

Albee, Edward	*Zoo Story*
Anonymous	*Everyman*
Aristophanes	*Lysistrata*
Beckett, Samuel	*Waiting for Godot*
Bolt, Robert	*Man for All Seasons*
Brecht, Bertolt	*Mother Courage and Her Children: A Chronicle of the Thirty Years War*
Chekhov, Anton	*Cherry Orchard*
Congreve, William	*Way of the World*
Durrenmatt, Friedrich	*Visit*
Fry, Christopher	*Lady's Not for Burning: A Comedy*
Genet, Jean	*Blacks, a Clown Show*
Gibson, William	*Miracle Worker; a Play for Television*
Giraudoux, Jean	*Madwoman of Chaillot*
Gorky, Maxim	*Lower Depths*
Hansberry, Lorraine	*Raisin in the Sun*
Hellman, Lillian	*Little Foxes*
Hochhuth, Rolf	*Deputy*
Ibsen, Henrik	*Doll's House*
Ionesco, Eugene	*Rhinoceros*
Jonson, Ben	*Volpone*
Lawrence, Jerome, and Robert E. Lee	*Inherit the Wind*
Lorca, Federico Garcia	*Blood Wedding*
McCullers, Carson	*Member of the Wedding*
MacLeish, Archibald	*J.B.*

Marlowe, Christopher	*Doctor Faustus*
Miller, Arthur	*Death of a Salesman*
Molière, Jean	*Misanthrope*
O'Casey, Sean	*Juno and the Paycock*
O'Neill, Eugene	*Long Day's Journey into Night*
Osborne, John	*Look Back in Anger, a Play in Three Acts*
Pinter, Harold	*Birthday Party*
Pirandello, Luigi	*Six Characters in Search of an Author*
Racine, Jean Baptiste	*Phaedra*
Rice, Tim, and Andrew Lloyd Webber	*Jesus Christ, Superstar*
Shakespeare, William	*Macbeth*
Shakespeare, William	*Midsummer Night's Dream*
Shaw, George Bernard	*Saint Joan*
Sheridan, Richard B.	*School for Scandal*
Sophocles	*Oedipus the King*
Strindberg, August	*Miss Julie*
Synge, John Millington	*Playboy of the Western World*
Wilde, Oscar	*Importance of Being Earnest*
Wilder, Thornton	*Our Town*
Williams, Tennessee	*Glass Menagerie*
Zindel, Paul	*Effect of Gamma Rays on Man-in-the-Moon Marigolds, a Drama in Two Acts*

1982 □ BIOGRAPHY

Angelou, Maya	*I Know Why the Caged Bird Sings*
Atkinson, Linda	*Mother Jones: The Most Dangerous Woman in America*
Banks, Lynne Reid	*Dark Quartet: The Story of the Brontës*
Brown, Claude	*Manchild in the Promised Land*
Carpenter, Humphrey	*Tolkien: A Biography*
Carrighar, Sally	*Home to the Wilderness*
Douglas, William O.	*Go East, Young Man: The Early Years; the Autobiography of William O. Douglas*
Frank, Anne	*Anne Frank: The Diary of a Young Girl*

Gunther, John — *Death Be Not Proud: A Memoir*

Gurko, Miriam — *Ladies of Seneca Falls: The Birth of the Woman's Rights Movement*

Hellman, Lillian — *Three: An Unfinished Woman, Pentimento, Scoundrel Time*

Herriot, James — *All Creatures Great and Small*

Johnson, Edgar — *Charles Dickens, His Tragedy and Triumph*

Keller, Helen Adams — *Story of My Life*

Kingston, Maxine Hong — *Woman Warrior: Memoirs of a Girlhood among Ghosts*

Klein, Joe — *Woody Guthrie: A Life*

Lash, Joseph P. — *Eleanor and Franklin: The Story of Their Relationship, Based on Eleanor Roosevelt's Private Papers*

McClellan, David — *Karl Marx: His Life and Thought*

Mead, Margaret — *Blackberry Winter: My Earlier Years*

Miller, Merle — *Plain Speaking: An Oral Biography of Harry S. Truman*

Morison, Samuel Eliot — *Christopher Columbus, Mariner*

Neihardt, John G. — *Black Elk Speaks: Being the Life Story of a Holy Man of the Oglala Sioux*

O'Keeffe, Georgia — *Georgia O'Keeffe*

Panov, Valery, and George Feifer — *To Dance*

Pardy, Anne — *Tisha: The Story of a Young Teacher in the Alaska Wilderness*

Poitier, Sidney — *This Life*

Rather, Dan, with Mickey Herskowitz — *Camera Never Blinks: Adventures of a TV Journalist*

Russell, Bill, and Taylor Branch — *Second Wind: The Memoirs of an Opinionated Man*

Sandburg, Carl — *Abraham Lincoln: The Prairie Years and the War Years*

Stein, Gertrude — *Autobiography of Alice B. Toklas*

Wolfe, Bertram David — *Three Who Made a Revolution: A Biographical History*

Wright, Richard — *Black Boy: A Record of Childhood and Youth*

X, Malcolm — *Autobiography of Malcolm X*

1982 □ DANCE

Ames, Jerry, and Jim Siegelman	*Book of Tap: Recovering America's Long Lost Dance*
Balanchine, George, and Francis Mason	*101 Stories of the Great Ballets*
Banes, Sally	*Terpsichore in Sneakers: Post-Modern Dance*
Cook, Susan	*Alvin Ailey American Dance Theater*
De Mille, Agnes	*American Dances*
Louis, Murray	*Inside Dance: Essays*
McDonagh, Don	*Complete Guide to Modern Dance*
Maiorano, Robert	*Worlds Apart: The Autobiography of a Dancer from Brooklyn*
Neale, Wendy	*On Your Toes: Beginning Ballet*
Philip, Richard, and Mary Whitney	*Danseur: The Male in Ballet*
Reynolds, Nancy (ed.)	*Dance Catalog*
Sorine, Daniel S., and Stephanie Riva Sorine	*Dancershoes*

1982 □ FICTION

Austen, Jane	*Pride and Prejudice*
Baldwin, James	*If Beale Street Could Talk*
Borland, Hal	*When the Legends Die*
Bradbury, Ray	*Martian Chronicles*
Brontë, Charlotte	*Jane Eyre*
Brontë, Emily	*Wuthering Heights*
Camus, Albert	*Plague*
Cather, Willa	*My Antonia*
Conrad, Joseph	*Lord Jim*
Crane, Stephen	*Red Badge of Courage*
Dickens, Charles	*Tale of Two Cities*
Dostoevsky, Fyodor	*Crime and Punishment*
Doyle, Arthur Conan	*Adventures of Sherlock Holmes*

Du Maurier, Daphne	*Rebecca*
Ellison, Ralph	*Invisible Man*
Faulkner, William	*Bear*
Finney, Jack	*Time and Again*
Fitzgerald, F. Scott	*Great Gatsby*
Golding, William	*Lord of the Flies*
Hardy, Thomas	*Far from the Madding Crowd*
Hawthorne, Nathaniel	*Scarlet Letter*
Heller, Joseph	*Catch-22*
Hemingway, Ernest	*Farewell to Arms*
Herbert, Frank	*Dune*
Hersey, John	*Wall*
Hesse, Hermann	*Siddhartha*
Huxley, Aldous	*Brave New World*
Joyce, James	*Portrait of the Artist as a Young Man*
Kesey, Ken	*One Flew over the Cuckoo's Nest*
Knowles, John	*Separate Peace*
Le Guin, Ursula K.	*Left Hand of Darkness*
Lee, Harper	*To Kill a Mockingbird*
McCullers, Carson	*Heart Is a Lonely Hunter*
Malamud, Bernard	*Fixer*
O'Brien, Tim	*Going after Cacciato: A Novel*
Olsen, Tillie	*Tell Me a Riddle*
Orwell, George	*Animal Farm*
Paton, Alan	*Cry, the Beloved Country*
Poe, Edgar Allan	*Fall of the House of Usher and Other Tales*
Remarque, Erich Maria	*All Quiet on the Western Front*
Salinger, J. D.	*Catcher in the Rye*
Singer, Isaac Bashevis	*Slave*
Solzhenitsyn, Alexander	*One Day in the Life of Ivan Denisovich*
Steinbeck, John	*Of Mice and Men*
Stoker, Bram	*Dracula*
Tolkien, J. R. R.	*Lord of the Rings*
Tolstoy, Leo	*War and Peace*
Twain, Mark	*Adventures of Huckleberry Finn*

Vonnegut, Kurt   *Slaughterhouse Five; or, The Children's Crusade*

Wharton, William   *Birdy*

1982 □ FILM/TELEVISION

Bobker, Lee R.   *Elements of Film*
Brownlow, Kevin   *Hollywood: The Pioneers*
Canutt, Yakima   *Stunt Man: The Autobiography of Yakima Canutt*

Comp. by the Editors of Super 0   *Film Maker's Guide to Super 8; The*
  Filmaker Magazine   *"How-to-Do-It" Book for Beginning and Advanced Film Makers*

Halas, John, and Roger Manvell   *Technique of Film Animation*
London, Mel   *Getting into Film*
Price, Jonathan   *Video Visions: A Medium Discovers Itself*
Rosenblum, Ralph, and Robert   *When the Shooting Stops . . . the Cutting*
  Karen   *Begins: A Film Editor's Story*
Shanks, Bob   *Cool Fire: How to Make It in Television*

1982 □ MUSIC

Copland, Aaron   *What to Listen For in Music*
Davies, Hunter   *Beatles*
Gaillard, Frye   *Watermelon Wine: The Spirit of Country Music*

Hurd, Michael   *Orchestra*
Miller, Jim (ed.)   *Rolling Stone Illustrated History of Rock and Roll*

Pavarotti, Luciano   *Pavarotti, My Own Story*
Roberts, John Storm   *Latin Tinge: The Impact of Latin American Music on the United States*

Rogers, Kenny, and Len Epand   *Making It with Music: Kenny Rogers' Guide to the Music Business*

Ruttencutter, Helen Drees   *Pianist's Progress*
Stokes, Geoffrey   *Star-Making Machinery: Inside the Business of Rock and Roll*

Van Ryzin, Lani   *Starting Your Own Band*

1982 □ NONFICTION

Agee, James, and Walker Evans	*Let Us Now Praise Famous Men*
Ballou, Robert O. (ed.)	*Portable World Bible*
Bell, Ruth	*Changing Bodies, Changing Lives: A Book for Teens on Sex and Relationships*
Benedict, Ruth Fulton	*Patterns of Culture*
Brand, Stewart (ed.)	*Next Whole Earth Catalog: Access to Tools*
Brecher, Edward M., and Consumer Reports Editors	*Licit and Illicit Drugs: The Consumers Union Report*
Bronowski, Jacob	*Ascent of Man*
Brown, Dee	*Bury My Heart at Wounded Knee: An Indian History of the American West*
Brown, Michael H.	*Laying Waste: The Poisoning of America by Toxic Chemicals*
Ceram, C. W.	*Gods, Graves, and Scholars: The Story of Archaeology*
Cooke, Alistair	*Alistair Cooke's America*
Covelli, Pat	*Borrowing Time: Growing Up with Juvenile Diabetes*
Crawford, Alan	*Thunder on the Right: The New Right and the Politics of Resentment*
Durant, William J.	*Story of Philosophy*
Ebenstein, William, and Edwin Fogelman	*Today's Isms: Communism, Fascism, Capitalism, Socialism*
Eisely, Loren	*Darwin's Century: Evolution and the Men Who Discovered It*
Fuller, R. Buckminster	*Operating Manual for Spaceship Earth*
Hamilton, Edith	*Mythology*
Hanckel, Frances, and John Cunningham	*Way of Love, a Way of Life: A Young Person's Introduction to What It Means to Be Gay*
Harding, Vincent	*There Is a River: The Black Struggle for Freedom in America*
Hayden, Torey L.	*One Child*

Heilbroner, Robert L.	*Worldly Philosophers: The Lives, Times and Ideas of the Great Economic Thinkers*
Hentoff, Nat	*First Freedom: The Tumultuous History of Free Speech in America*
Hofstadter, Douglas R.	*Gödel, Escher, Bach: An Eternal Golden Braid*
Homer	*Odyssey of Homer: A Modern Translation*
Hoyt, Patricia	*How to Get Started When You Don't Know Where to Begin*
Japan Broadcasting Corp. (ed.)	*Unforgettable Fire: Pictures Drawn by Atomic Bomb Survivors*
Jenkins, Peter	*Walk across America*
Johanson, Donald C., and Maitland A. Edey	*Lucy: The Beginnings of Human Kind*
Jones, Landon Y.	*Great Expectations: America and the Baby Boom Generation*
Jungk, Robert	*Brighter than a Thousand Suns: A Personal History of the Atomic Scientists*
Larrick, Nancy (ed.)	*Crazy to Be Alive in Such a Strange World: Poems about People*
Levine, Suzanne, and Harriet Lyons	*Decade of Women: A Ms. History of the Seventies in Words and Pictures*
Lorenz, Konrad	*On Aggression*
Manchester, William	*Glory and the Dream: A Narrative History of America, 1932–1972*
Mead, Margaret	*Culture and Commitment: The New Relationships between the Generations in the 1970's*
Meltzer, Milton	*Never to Forget: The Jews of the Holocaust*
Mirkin, Gabe, and Marshall Hoffman	*Sportsmedicine Book*
Redman, Eric	*Dance of Legislation*
Sagan, Carl	*Cosmos*
Santoli, Al (ed.)	*Everything We Had: An Oral History of the Vietnam War by Thirty-three American Soldiers Who Fought It*
Schlesinger, M. Arthur	*Imperial Presidency*

Terkel, Studs	*Working: People Talk about What They Do All Day and How They Feel about What They Do*
Thomas, Lewis	*Lives of a Cell: Notes of a Biology Watcher*
Thoreau, Henry David	*Walden and Civil Disobedience*
Timerman, Jacobo	*Prisoner without a Name, Cell without a Number*
Tocqueville, Alexis de	*Democracy in America*
Toffler, Alvin	*Third Wave*
Watson, James D. and Guntor S. Stent (ed.)	*Double Helix: A Personal Account of the Discovery of the Structure of DNA*

1982 □ PERFORMING ARTS

Baird, Bil	*Art of the Puppet*
Barton, Peter	*Staying Power: Performing Artists Talk about Their Lives*
Billington, Michael (ed.)	*Performing Arts: An Illustrated Guide*
Campbell, Patricia J.	*Passing the Hat: Street Performers in America*
Hamblin, Kay	*Mime: A Playbook of Silent Fantasy*
Page, Patrick	*Big Book of Magic*
Towsen, John H.	*Clowns*

1982 □ THEATER

Gottfried, Martin	*Broadway Musicals*
Hagen, Uta, and Haskel Frankel	*Respect for Acting*
Hanff, Helene	*Underfoot in Show Business*
Hoggett, Chris	*Stage Crafts*
Lewis, Robert	*Advice to the Players*
Matson, Katinka	*Working Actor: A Guide to the Profession*
Olfson, Lewy (ed.)	*Fifty Great Scenes for Student Actors*
Seto, Judith Roberts (ed.)	*Young Actor's Workbook*
Stanislavsky, Konstantin	*Actor Prepares*

1988 □ ART, ARCHITECTURE, AND PHOTOGRAPHY

Adams, Ansel, and Mary Street Alinder	*Ansel Adams, an Autobiography*
Allen, Edward	*How Buildings Work: The Natural Order of Architecture*
DeCarava, Roy, and Langston Hughes	*Sweet Flypaper of Life*
Hamilton, George Heard	*Painting and Sculpture in Europe, 1880–1940*
Hibbard, Howard	*Michelangelo*
Krauss, Rosalind E.	*Passages in Modern Sculpture*
Salvadori, Mario George	*Why Buildings Stand Up: The Strength of Architecture*

1988 □ BIOGRAPHY

Angelou, Maya	*I Know Why the Caged Bird Sings*
Benson, Jackson J.	*True Adventures of John Steinbeck, Writer: A Biography*
Carpenter, Humphrey	*Tolkien: A Biography*
Clark, Ronald W.	*Freud: The Man and the Cause*
Douglas, William O.	*Court Years, 1939–1975: The Autobiography of William O. Douglas*
Douglas, William O.	*Go East, Young Man: The Early Years; the Autobiography of William O. Douglas*
Egan, Eileen	*Such a Vision of the Street: Mother Teresa—the Spirit and the Work*
Fox, Stephen R.	*John Muir and His Legacy: The American Conservation Movement*
Frank, Anne	*Anne Frank: The Diary of a Young Girl*
French, A. P. (ed.)	*Einstein: A Centenary Volume*
Furlong, Monica	*Merton: A Biography*
Gill, Derek L. T.	*Quest: The Life of Elizabeth Kubler-Ross*
Griffith, Elisabeth	*In Her Own Right: The Life of Elizabeth Cady Stanton*
Gunther, John	*Death Be Not Proud: A Memoir*
Hellman, Lillian	*Three: An Unfinished Woman, Pentimento, Scoundrel Time*

Herriot, James	*All Creatures Great and Small*
Keller, Helen Adams	*Story of My Life*
Kingston, Maxine Hong	*Woman Warrior: Memoirs of a Girlhood among Ghosts*
Klein, Joe	*Woody Guthrie: A Life*
Lash, Joseph P.	*Eleanor and Franklin: The Story of Their Relationship, Based on Eleanor Roosevelt's Private Papers*
Manchester, William	*Last Lion: Winston Spencer Churchill*
Mandela, Winnie	*Part of My Soul Went with Him*
Marius, Richard	*Thomas More: A Biography*
Mead, Margaret	*Blackberry Winter: My Earlier Years*
Miller, Merle	*Plain Speaking: An Oral Biography of Harry S. Truman*
Morgan, Ted	*FDR: A Biography*
Neihardt, John G.	*Black Elk Speaks: Being the Life Story of a Holy Man of the Oglala Sioux*
Oates, Stephen B.	*Let the Trumpet Sound: The Life of Martin Luther King, Jr.*
O'Keeffe, Georgia	*Georgia O'Keeffe*
Oshinsky, David M.	*Conspiracy So Immense: The World of Joe McCarthy*
Page, Joseph A.	*Peron: A Biography*
Sandburg, Carl	*Abraham Lincoln: The Prairie Years and the War Years*
Shevchenko, Arkady N.	*Breaking with Moscow*
Smith, Denis Mack	*Mussolini*
Stein, Gertrude	*Autobiography of Alice B. Toklas*
Wexler, Alice	*Emma Goldman: An Intimate Life*
Wolfe, Bertram David	*Three Who Made a Revolution: A Biographical History*
Woods, Donald	*Biko*
Wright, Richard	*Black Boy: A Record of Childhood and Youth*
X, Malcolm	*Autobiography of Malcolm X*
Yeager, Chuck, and Leo Janos	*Yeager: An Autobiography*

1988 □ DANCE

Ames, Jerry, and Jim Siegelman	*Book of Tap: Recovering America's Long Lost Dance*
Balanchine, George, and Francis Mason	*101 Stories of the Great Ballets*
Bentley, Toni	*Winter Season: A Dancer's Journal*
Bland, Alexander, and John Percival	*Men Dancing: Performers and Performances*
Coe, Robert	*Dance in America*
Emery, Lynne Fauley	*Black Dance in the United States: From 1619 to 1970*
Stearns, Marshall, and Jean Stearns	*Jazz Dance: The Story of American Vernacular Dance*

1988 □ FICTION

Austen, Jane	*Pride and Prejudice*
Baldwin, James	*Go Tell It on the Mountain*
Bradbury, Ray	*Fahrenheit 451*
Brin, David	*Postman*
Brontë, Charlotte	*Jane Eyre*
Cather, Willa	*My Antonia*
Cormier, Robert	*Chocolate War*
Crane, Stephen	*Red Badge of Courage*
Dickens, Charles	*Tale of Two Cities*
Dostoevsky, Fyodor	*Crime and Punishment*
Doyle, Arthur Conan	*Adventures of Sherlock Holmes*
Emecheta, Buchi	*Bride Price*
Faulkner, William	*Reivers: A Reminiscence*
Finney, Jack	*Time and Again*
Fitzgerald, F. Scott	*Great Gatsby*
Gaines, Ernest J.	*Autobiography of Miss Jane Pittman*
Gardner, John	*Grendel*
Golding, William	*Lord of the Flies*
Guest, Judith	*Ordinary People*
Hawthorne, Nathaniel	*Scarlet Letter*
Heller, Joseph	*Catch-22*

Hesse, Hermann	*Siddhartha*
Huxley, Aldous	*Brave New World*
Keneally, Thomas	*Schindler's List*
Le Guin, Ursula K.	*Left Hand of Darkness*
Lee, Harper	*To Kill a Mockingbird*
Lord, Bette B.	*Spring Moon: A Novel of China*
McCullers, Carson	*Heart Is a Lonely Hunter*
McKinley, Robin	*Beauty*
Malamud, Bernard	*Fixer*
Markandaya, Kamala	*Nectar in a Sieve*
Mishima, Yukio	*Sound of Waves*
O'Brien, Tim	*Going after Cacciato: A Novel*
Orwell, George	*Animal Farm*
Paton, Alan	*Cry, the Beloved Country*
Poe, Edgar Allan	*Tales of Terror: Ten Short Stories*
Potok, Chaim	*Chosen*
Remarque, Erich Maria	*All Quiet on the Western Front*
Salinger, J. D.	*Catcher in the Rye*
Shange, Ntozake	*Betsey Brown*
Sinclair, Upton	*Jungle*
Singer, Isaac Bashevis	*Collected Stories of Isaac Bashevis Singer*
Solzhenitsyn, Alexander	*One Day in the Life of Ivan Denisovich*
Steinbeck, John	*Grapes of Wrath*
Stoker, Bram	*Dracula*
Thomas, Dylan	*Portrait of the Artist as a Young Dog*
Tolkien, J. R. R.	*Lord of the Rings*
Twain, Mark	*Adventures of Huckleberry Finn*
Vonnegut, Kurt	*Slaughterhouse Five; or, The Children's Crusade*
Welch, James	*Fools Crow*
Willard, Nancy	*Things Invisible to See*
Wright, Richard	*Native Son*

1988 □ FILM/TELEVISION

Brownlow, Kevin	*Hollywood: The Pioneers*
Ellerbee, Linda	*And So It Goes*
Gish, Lillian	*Movies, Mr. Griffith and Me*
Kael, Pauline	*Citizen Kane Book: Raising Kane*
Rosenblum, Ralph, and Robert Karen	*When the Shooting Stops . . . the Cutting Begins: A Film Editor's Story*
Sperber, Ann M.	*Murrow: His Life and Times*
Wiley, Mason, and Damien Boda	*Inside Oscar: The Unofficial History of the Academy Award*

1988 □ MUSIC

Brown, James, and Bruce Tucker	*James Brown: The Godfather of Soul*
Hart, Philip	*Conductors: A New Generation*
Hirshey, Gerri	*Nowhere to Run: The Story of Soul Music*
Marsh, Dave	*Glory Days: Bruce Springsteen in the 1980's*
Mason, Michael (ed.)	*Country Music Book*
Mordden, Ethan	*Demented: The World of the Opera Diva*
Schonberg, Harold C.	*Glorious Ones: Classical Music's Legendary Performers*
Wade, Graham	*Segovia: A Celebration of the Man and His Music*
Ward, Ed, Geoffrey Stokes, and Ken Tucker	*Rock of Ages: The Rolling Stone History of Rock and Roll*
Zinsser, William	*Willie and Dwike: An American Profile*

1988 □ NONFICTION

Agee, James, and Walker Evans	*Let Us Now Praise Famous Men*
Ballou, Robert O. (ed.)	*Portable World Bible*
Bell, Ruth	*Changing Bodies, Changing Lives: A Book for Teens on Sex and Relationships*
Black Veterans and Terry Wallace (ed.)	*Bloods: An Oral History of the Vietnam War*

Bowen, Catherine Drinker	*Miracle at Philadelphia: The Story of the Constitutional Convention, May to September, 1787*
Bronowski, Jacob	*Ascent of Man*
Brown, Dee	*Bury My Heart at Wounded Knee: An Indian History of the American West*
Brown, Michael H.	*Laying Waste: The Poisoning of America by Toxic Chemicals*
Carson, Rachel	*Silent Spring*
Ceram, C. W.	*Gods, Graves, and Scholars: The Story of Archaeology*
Durant, William J.	*Story of Philosophy*
Ebenstein, William, and Edwin Fogelman	*Today's Isms: Communism, Fascism, Capitalism, Socialism*
Eisely, Loren	*Darwin's Century: Evolution and the Men Who Discovered It*
Friedan, Betty	*Feminine Mystique*
Hamilton, Edith	*Mythology*
Harding, Vincent	*There Is a River: The Black Struggle for Freedom in America*
Heilbroner, Robert L.	*Worldly Philosophers: The Lives, Times and Ideas of the Great Economic Thinkers*
Hersey, John	*Hiroshima*
Johanson, Donald C., and Maitland A. Edey	*Lucy: The Beginnings of Human Kind*
Johnson, Paul	*Modern Times: The World from the Twenties to the Eighties*
Langone, John	*Violence! Our Fastest Growing Public Health Problem*
Least Heat Moon, William	*Blue Highways: A Journey into America*
Lelyveld, Joseph	*Move Your Shadow: South Africa Black and White*
Lopez, Barry	*Arctic Dreams: Imagination and Desire in a Northern Landscape*
Lorenz, Konrad	*On Aggression*
Lukas, J. Anthony	*Common Ground: A Turbulent Decade in the Lives of Three American Families*
Malcolm, Andrew H.	*Final Harvest: An American Tragedy*

Meltzer, Milton	*Ain't Gonna Study War No More: The Story of America's Peace Seekers*
Meltzer, Milton	*Never to Forget: The Jews of the Holocaust*
Naisbitt, John	*Megatrends: Ten New Directions Transforming Our Lives*
Postman, Neil	*Amusing Ourselves to Death: Public Discourse in the Age of Show Business*
Raines, Howell	*My Soul Is Rested: Movement Days in the Deep South Remembered*
Santoli, Al	*To Bear Any Burden: The Vietnam War and Its Aftermath in the Words of Americans and Southeast Asians*
Schank, Roger C., with Peter G. Childers	*Cognitive Computer: On Language, Learning, and Artificial Intelligence*
Schell, Jonathan	*Fate of the Earth*
Thomas, Lewis	*Lives of a Cell: Notes of a Biology Watcher*
Tocqueville, Alexis de	*Democracy in America*
Uhlig, Mark A. (ed.)	*Apartheid in Crisis*
Watson, James D., and Guntor S. Stent (ed.)	*Double Helix: A Personal Account of the Discovery of the Structure of DNA*
Weiss, Ann E.	*Good Neighbors? The United States and Latin America*
Wolfe, Tom	*Right Stuff*
Wyden, Peter	*Day One: Before Hiroshima and After*
Zerman, Melvyn Bernard	*Taking on the Press: Constitutional Rights in Conflict*

1988 ☐ POETRY

Amis, Kingsley (ed.)	*New Oxford Book of Light Verse*
Dickinson, Emily	*Final Harvest: Emily Dickinson's Poems*
Randall, Dudley (ed.)	*Black Poets*
Rexroth, Kenneth (ed.)	*One Hundred Poems from the Japanese*
Untermeyer, Louis (ed.)	*Fifty Modern American and British Poets, 1920–1970*
Yevtushenko, Yevgeny	*Poetry of Yevgeny Yevtushenko*

1988 □ RELATED ARTS

Blackstone Jr., Harry — *Blackstone Book of Magic and Illusion*
Goldberg, RoseLee — *Performance: Live Art 1909 to the Present*
Sharaff, Irene — *Broadway to Hollywood: Costumes Designed by Irene Sharaff*

1988 □ THEATER

Albee, Edward — *Zoo Story*
Aristophanes — *Lysistrata*
Bernstein, Leonard — *West Side Story*
Bordman, Gerald — *American Musical Comedy: From Adonis to Dreamgirls*

Brandreth, Gyles — *Great Theatrical Disasters*
Chekhov, Anton — *Cherry Orchard*
Coward, Noel — *Blithe Spirit*
Eliot, T. S. — *Murder in the Cathedral*
Hart, Moss — *Act One*
Hellman, Lillian — *Children's Hour*
Henderson, Mary C. — *Theatre in America: Two Hundred Years of Plays, Players and Productions*

Ibsen, Henrik — *Doll's House*
Kander, John — *Cabaret*
Kaufman, George S., and Moss Hart — *You Can't Take It with You*

Lerner, Alan Jay — *Musical Theatre: A Celebration*
MacDermot, Galt — *Hair*
Medoff, Mark — *Children of a Lesser God*
Miller, Arthur — *Price*
Molière, Jean — *Le Bourgeois Gentilhomme*
Ndlovu, Duma (ed.) — *Woza Afrika: An Anthology of South African Plays*

O'Neill, Eugene — *Long Day's Journey into Night*
Pirandello, Luigi — *Six Characters in Search of an Author*
Rodgers, Richard — *Pal Joey*
Rodgers, Richard, and Oscar Hammerstein — *Oklahoma!*

Rostand, Edmond   *Cyrano de Bergerac*

Sartre, Jean Paul   *No Exit*

Shakespeare, William   *Romeo and Juliet*

Shakespeare, William   *Tempest*

Shakespeare, William   *Twelfth Night*

Shaw, George Bernard   *Arms and the Man*

Shaw, George Bernard   *Pygmalion*

Sheridan, Richard B.   *School for Scandal*

Shewey, Don, and Susan Schacter   *Caught in the Act*

Simon, Neil   *Brighton Beach Memoirs*

Sondheim, Stephen   *Sweeney Todd: The Demon Barber of Fleet Street*

Sophocles   *Oedipus the King*

Stanislavsky, Konstantin   *Actor Prepares*

Sullivan, Arthur   *Pirates of Penzance*

Waley, Arthur (tr.)   *Noh Drama: Ten Plays from the Japanese Fourteenth and Fifteenth Centuries*

Weill, Kurt   *Threepenny Opera*

Wickham, Glynne W.   *History of the Theatre*

Wilde, Oscar   *Importance of Being Earnest*

Wilder, Thornton   *Our Town*

Williams, Tennessee   *Streetcar Named Desire*

1991 □ ART, ARCHITECTURE, AND PHOTOGRAPHY

Allen, Edward   *How Buildings Work: The Natural Order of Architecture*

Czarnecki, Joseph P.   *Last Traces: The Lost Art of Auschwitz*

DeCarava, Roy, and Langston Hughes   *Sweet Flypaper of Life*

Duncan, Alastair   *American Art Deco*

Finn, David   *How to Look at Sculpture*

Greenough, Sara   *On the Art of Fixing a Shadow: 150 Years of Photography*

Hartt, Frederick   *Art: A History of Painting, Sculpture, and Architecture*

Heller, Nancy G.   *Women Artists: An Illustrated History*

                           More Joy of Photography

Livingston, Jane	*Odyssey: The Art of Photography at National Geographic*
Mangelson, Tom	*Images of Nature*
Salvadori, Mario George	*Why Buildings Stand Up: The Strength of Architecture*
Stern, Robert	*Modern Classicism*
Updike, John	*Just Looking: Essays on Art*
Vlach, John Michael	*Plain Painters: Making Sense of American Folk Art*
Weaver, Mike	*Art of Photography, 1839–1989*

1991 ☐ BIOGRAPHY

Baker, Russell	*Growing Up*
Barry, Kathleen L.	*Susan B. Anthony—Biography of a Singular Feminist*
Cheng, Nien	*Life and Death in Shanghai*
Comer, James P.	*Maggie's American Dream: The Life and Times of a Black Family*
Conway, Jill Ker	*Road from Coorain*
Curie, Eve	*Madame Curie; a Biography*
Dillard, Annie	*American Childhood*
Gies, Miep, with Alison Leslie Gold	*Anne Frank Remembered: The Story of the Woman Who Helped to Hide the Frank Family*
Hayslip, Le Ly, and Jay Wurts	*When Heaven and Earth Changed Places: A Vietnamese Woman's Journey from War to Peace*
Kazimiroff, Theodore L.	*Last Algonquin*
Kovic, Ron	*Born on the Fourth of July*
Lovell, Mary S.	*Sound of Wings: The Biography of Amelia Earhart*
Lyttle, Richard B.	*Pablo Picasso: The Man and the Image*
MacNeil, Robert	*Wordstruck: A Memoir*
Martin, Ralph	*Golda: Golda Meir's Romantic Years*
Mathabane, Mark	*Kaffir Boy: The True Story of a Black Youth's Coming of Age in Apartheid South Africa*
Mathews, Jay	*Escalante: The Best Teacher in America*

Mehta, Ved	*Sound Shadows of the New World*
Miller, Merle	*Plain Speaking: An Oral Biography of Harry S. Truman*
Mills, Judie	*John F. Kennedy*
Morgan, Sally	*My Place*
Mowat, Farley	*Woman in the Mists: The Story of Dian Fossey and the Mountain Gorillas of Africa*
Oppenheimer, Judy	*Private Demons: The Life of Shirley Jackson*
Robeson, Susan	*Whole World in His Hands: A Pictorial Biography of Paul Robeson*
Robinson, Roxana	*Georgia O'Keeffe: A Life*
Salerno-Sonnenberg, Nadja	*Nadja, on My Way*
Sender, Ruth Minsky	*Cage*
Sharf, Lois	*Eleanor Roosevelt: First Lady of American Liberalism*
Sunstein, Emily W.	*Mary Shelley: Romance and Reality*
Van Devanter, Lynda, and Christopher Morgan	*Home before Morning*
Von Staden, Wendelgard	*Darkness over the Valley*
Witherspoon, William Roger	*Martin Luther King, Jr.: To the Mountaintop*
Wolff, Tobias	*This Boy's Life: A Memoir*
Wright, Richard	*Black Boy: A Record of Childhood and Youth*

1991 □ DANCE

Balanchine, George, and Francis Mason	*101 Stories of the Great Ballets*
Bentley, Toni	*Winter Season: A Dancer's Journal*
Bland, Alexander, and John Percival	*Men Dancing: Performers and Performances*
Clarke, Mary, and Clement Crisp	*Ballerina: The Art of Women in Classical Ballet*
Coe, Robert	*Dance in America*
Fraser, John	*Private View: Inside Baryshnikov's American Ballet Theatre*

Gruen, John — *People Who Dance: Twenty-two Dancers Tell Their Own Stories*

Haskins, James — *Black Dance in America: A History through Its People*

Stearns, Marshall, and Jean Stearns — *Jazz Dance: The Story of American Vernacular Dance*

1991 □ FICTION

Achebe, Chinua	*Things Fall Apart*
Anaya, Rudolfo A.	*Bless Me, Ultima*
Austen, Jane	*Pride and Prejudice*
Bradbury, Ray	*Fahrenheit 451*
Brontë, Charlotte	*Jane Eyre*
Camus, Albert	*Stranger*
Doctorow, E. L.	*Ragtime*
Dorris, Michael	*Yellow Raft on Blue Water*
Doyle, Arthur Conan	*Adventures of Sherlock Holmes*
Faulkner, William	*Portable Faulkner*
Fitzgerald, F. Scott	*Great Gatsby*
Flaubert, Gustave	*Madame Bovary*
Gaines, Ernest J.	*Gathering of Old Men*
Golding, William	*Lord of the Flies*
Greenberg, Joanne	*Of Such Small Differences*
Hemingway, Ernest	*Farewell to Arms*
Hesse, Hermann	*Siddhartha*
Joyce, James	*Portrait of the Artist as a Young Man*
Keneally, Thomas	*Chant of Jimmie Blacksmith*
Lee, Harper	*To Kill a Mockingbird*
London, Jack	*Call of the Wild*
McCullers, Carson	*Member of the Wedding*
Malamud, Bernard	*Fixer*
Mason, Bobbie Anne	*In Country*
Morrison, Toni	*Beloved*
O'Connor, Flannery	*Everything That Rises Must Converge*
Paton, Alan	*Cry, the Beloved Country*
Potok, Chaim	*Chosen*

Renault, Mary   *King Must Die*

Salinger, J. D.   *Catcher in the Rye*

Solzhenitsyn, Alexander   *One Day in the Life of Ivan Denisovich*

Steinbeck, John   *East of Eden*

Tan, Amy   *Joy Luck Club*

Tevis, Walter S.   *Queen's Gambit*

Tolkien, J. R. R.   *Lord of the Rings*

Twain, Mark   *Adventures of Huckleberry Finn*

Tyler, Anne   *Accidental Tourist*

Vidal, Gore   *Lincoln: A Novel*

White, T. H.   *Once and Future King*

1991 □ FILM/TELEVISION

Bogle, Donald   *Toms, Coons, Mulattoes, Mammies and Bucks: An Interpretative History of Blacks in American Films*

Brownlow, Kevin   *Hollywood: The Pioneers*

Finch, Christopher   *Art of Walt Disney: From Mickey Mouse to the Magic Kingdoms*

Searles, Baird   *Films of Science Fiction and Fantasy*

Sennett, Ted   *Art of Hanna-Barbera: Fifty Years of Creativity*

1991 □ MUSIC

Crowther, Bruce, and Mike Pinfold   *Big Band Years*

Haskins, James   *Black Music in America: A History through Its People*

Kernfeld, Barry (ed.)   *New Grove Dictionary of Jazz*

Miller, Jim (ed.)   *Rolling Stone Illustrated History of Rock and Roll*

Mordden, Ethan   *Demented: The World of the Opera Diva*

Schonberg, Harold C.   *Glorious Ones: Classical Music's Legendary Performers*

Smith, Joe   *Off the Record: An Oral History of Popular Music*

1991 □ NONFICTION

	Holy Bible: New Revised Standard Version
Allen, James Paul, and Eugene James Turner	*We the People: An Atlas of America's Ethnic Diversity*
Arendt, Hannah	*On Violence*
Betcher, William	*Intimate Play: Creating Romance in Everyday Life*
Bloom, Allan	*Closing of the American Mind*
Bolen, Jean Shinoda	*Goddesses in Everywoman: A New Psychology of Women*
Bolen, Jean Shinoda	*Gods in Everyman: A New Psychology of Men's Lives and Loves*
Borysenko, Joan	*Minding the Body, Mending the Mind*
Boslough, John	*Stephen Hawking's Universe*
Bradshaw, John	*Bradshaw on the Family: A Revolutionary Way of Self-Discovery*
Burstein, Daniel	*Yen! Japan's New Financial Empire and Its Threat to America*
Caduto, Michael J., and Joseph Bruchac	*Keepers of the Earth: Native American Stories and Environmental Activities for Children*
Campbell, Joseph	*Power of Myth*
Child, Julia	*Way to Cook*
Earth Works Group	*Fifty Simple Things You Can Do to Save the Earth*
FitzGerald, Frances	*Fire in the Lake: The Vietnamese and the Americans in Vietnam*
Fossey, Dian	*Gorillas in the Mist*
Funk, Wilfred John, and Norman Lewis	*Thirty Days to a More Powerful Vocabulary*
Gay, Kathlyn	*Greenhouse Effect*
Gonzales-Crussi, F.	*Five Senses*
Goodall, Jane	*In the Shadow of Man*
Hartman, William K.	*Cycles of Fire: Stars, Galaxies, and the Wonder of Deep Space*
Hawking, Stephen W.	*Brief History of Time: From the Big Bang to Black Holes*

Hirsch Jr., E. D.	*Cultural Literacy: What Every American Needs to Know*
Hirsch Jr., E. D. (ed.)	*First Dictionary of Cultural Literacy: What Our Children Need to Know*
Hyde, Dayton O.	*Don Coyote: The Good Times and Bad of a Maligned American Original*
Hyde, Margaret Oldroyd, and Elizabeth H. Forsyth	*Terrorism: A Special Kind of Violence*
Irwin, Constance H. Frick	*Strange Footprints on the Land: Vikings in America*
Jung, Carl Gustav	*Man and His Symbols*
Kesselman-Turkel, Judi, and Franklynn Peterson	*Getting It Down: How to Put Your Ideas on Paper*
Key, Wilson Bryan	*Media Sexploitation*
Kidder, Tracy	*Among Schoolchildren*
Kingston, Maxine Hong	*China Men*
Kitzinger, Sheila	*Being Born*
Kitzinger, Sheila	*Complete Book of Pregnancy and Childbirth*
Kozol, Jonathan	*Rachel and Her Children: Homeless Families in America*
Lelyveld, Joseph	*Move Your Shadow: South Africa Black and White*
Lewin, Roger	*Bones of Contention: Controversies in the Search for Human Origin*
Mabie, Margot	*Constitution: Reflection of a Changing Nation*
Macaulay, David	*Way Things Work*
McPhee, John	*In Suspect Terrain*
Madaras, Lynda, and Area Madaras	*What's Happening to My Body? Book for Boys: A Growing Up Guide for Parents and Sons*
Madaras, Lynda, and Area Madaras	*What's Happening to My Body? Book for Girls: A Growing Up Guide for Parents and Daughters*
Marrin, Albert	*War Clouds in the West: Indians and Cavalrymen, 1860–1890*

Meltzer, Milton	*Rescue: The Story of How Gentiles Saved Jews in the Holocaust*
Muench, David, and Donald G. Pike	*Anasazi: Ancient People of the Rock*
Parrot, Andrea	*Coping with Date Rape and Acquaintance Rape*
Peck, M. Scott	*Road Less Traveled*
Perl, Lila	*Hunter's Stew and Hangtown Fry: What Pioneer Americans Ate and Why*
Peters, Thomas J., and Robert H. Waterman Jr.	*In Search of Excellence: Lessons from America's Best Run Companies*
Roueche, Berton	*Medical Detectives*
Sagan, Carl	*Cosmos*
San Souci, Robert D.	*Loch Ness Monster: Opposing Viewpoints*
Shilts, Randy	*And the Band Played On: Politics, People, and the AIDS Epidemic*
Sinetar, Marsha	*Do What You Love, the Money Will Follow: Discovering Your Right Livelihood*
Steiner, Stan	*La Raza: The Mexican Americans*
U.S. Bureau of Labor Statistics	*Occupational Outlook Handbook*
Weiner, Jonathan	*Planet Earth*
Williams, Juan	*Eyes on the Prize: America's Civil Rights Years 1954–1965*
Woolger, Roger J.	*Other Lives, Other Selves: A Jungian Psychotherapist Discovers Past Lives*
Yolen, Jane (ed.)	*Favorite Folktales from Around the World*

1991 □ POETRY

Christopher, Nicholas (ed.)	*Under 35: The New Generation of American Poets*
Doreski, Carole, and William Doreski	*How to Read and Interpret Poetry*
Hall, Donald	*Best American Poetry*
Selected by Paul B. Janeczko	*Going Over to Your Place: Poems for Each Other*

1991 □ RELATED ARTS

Antekeier, Kristopher, and Greg Aunapu	*Ringmaster! My Year on the Road with "The Greatest Show on Earth"*
Took, Barry	*Comedy Greats: A Celebration of Comic Genius Past and Present*
Volpe, Tod M., and Beth Cathers	*Treasures of the American Arts and Crafts Movement, 1890–1920*

1991 □ THEATER

Aeschylus	*Agamemnon*
Anouilh, Jean	*Antigone*
Anouilh, Jean	*Lark*
Aristophanes	*Lysistrata*
Baldwin, James	*Amen Corner*
Beckett, Samuel	*Waiting for Godot*
Bordman, Gerald	*American Musical Comedy: From Adonis to Dreamgirls*
Brandreth, Gyles	*Great Theatrical Disasters*
Brecht, Bertolt	*Mother Courage and Her Children: A Chronicle of the Thirty Years War*
Chekhov, Anton	*Cherry Orchard*
Coward, Noel	*Blithe Spirit*
De Vega, Lope	*Sheep Well*
Fugard, Athol	*Master Harold and the Boys*
Giraudoux, Jean	*Madwoman of Chaillot*
Hansberry, Lorraine	*Raisin in the Sun*
Hart, Moss	*Act One*
Hellman, Lillian	*Children's Hour*
Henderson, Mary C.	*Theatre in America: Two Hundred Years of Plays, Players and Productions*
Henley, Beth	*Crimes of the Heart*
Herman, Jerry, and Michael Stewart	*Hello, Dolly!*
Ibsen, Henrik	*Doll's House*
Ionesco, Eugene	*Rhinoceros*
Jones, Tom	*Fantasticks*

Kaufman, George S., and Moss Hart	*You Can't Take It with You*
Lawrence, Robert Gilford	*Restoration Plays*
Lorca, Federico Garcia	*Blood Wedding*
MacLeish, Archibald	*J.B.*
Medoff, Mark	*Children of a Lesser God*
Miller, Arthur	*Crucible*
Molière, Jean	*Misanthrope*
O'Neill, Eugene	*Long Day's Journey into Night*
Pinter, Harold	*Birthday Party*
Pirandello, Luigi	*Six Characters in Search of an Author*
Pomerance, Bernard	*Elephant Man*
Rostand, Edmond	*Cyrano de Bergerac*
Sartre, Jean Paul	*No Exit*
Shaffer, Peter	*Equus*
Shakespeare, William	*King Lear*
Shaw, George Bernard	*Pygmalion*
Shaw, George Bernard	*Saint Joan*
Shepard, Sam	*Tooth of Crime: Geography of a Horse Dreamer*
Sheridan, Richard B.	*School for Scandal*
Simon, Neil	*Odd Couple*
Sophocles	*Oedipus the King*
Stanislavsky, Konstantin	*Actor Prepares*
Stoppard, Tom	*Rosencrantz and Guildenstern Are Dead*
Strindberg, August	*Miss Julie*
Synge, J. M.	*Riders to the Sea*
Webber, Andrew Lloyd	*Cats*
Wickham, Glynne W.	*History of the Theatre*
Wilde, Oscar	*Importance of Being Earnest*
Wilder, Thornton	*Matchmaker*
Williams, Tennessee	*Glass Menagerie*
Zindel, Paul	*Effect of Gamma Rays on Man-in-the-Moon Marigolds, a Drama in Two Acts*

1994 □ ART, ARCHITECTURE, AND PHOTOGRAPHY

Arnason, H. Horvard	*History of Modern Art: Painting, Sculpture, Architecture, Photography*
Arwas, Victor	*Art Deco*
Bearden, Romare, and Harry Henderson	*History of African-American Artists: From 1972 to the Present*
Finn, David	*How to Look at Sculpture*
Gassan, Arnold, and A. J. Meek	*Exploring Black and White Photography*
Gilbert, George	*Complete Photography Careers Handbook: Expanded to Include Electronic Imaging*
Goldberg, Vicki	*Power of Photography: How Photographs Changed Our Lives*
Hartt, Frederick	*Art: A History of Painting, Sculpture, and Architecture*
Harvey, Liz (ed.)	*Shoot! Everything You Ever Wanted to Know about 35mm Photography*
Hedgecoe, John	*Photographer's Handbook*
Heller, Nancy G.	*Women Artists: An Illustrated History*
Janson, H. W., and Anthony F. Janson	*History of Art*
Macaulay, David	*Castle*
Stern, Robert	*Modern Classicism*
Strickland, Carol	*Annotated Mona Lisa: A Crash Course in Art History from Prehistoric to Post-Modern*
Wade, Edwin L. (ed.)	*Arts of the North American Indian: Native Traditions in Evolution*

1994 □ BIOGRAPHY

Angelou, Maya	*I Know Why the Caged Bird Sings*
Ashe, Arthur, and Arnold Rampersad	*Days of Grace: A Memoir*
Baker, Russell	*Growing Up*
Brave Bird, Mary, and Richard Erdoes	*Lakota Woman*

Cantwell, Mary	*American Girl: Scenes from a Small-Town Childhood*
Clarke, Gerald	*Capote: A Biography*
Collier, James Lincoln	*Louis Armstrong: An American Success Story*
Conway, Jill Ker	*Road from Coorain*
Cook, Blanche Wiesen	*Eleanor Roosevelt: Vol. 1 1884–1932*
Criddle, Joan D., and Teeda Butt Mam	*To Destroy You Is No Loss: The Odyssey of a Cambodian Family*
Curie, Eve	*Madame Curie; a Biography*
De Mille, Agnes	*Dance to the Piper*
Delany, Sara, and A. Elizabeth Delaney with Amy Hill Hearth	*Having Our Say: The Delany Sisters' First One Hundred Years*
Gherman, Beverly	*E. B. White: Some Writer!*
Gies, Miep, with Alison Leslie Gold	*Anne Frank Remembered: The Story of the Woman Who Helped to Hide the Frank Family*
Kerr, M. E.	*Me Me Me Me Me: Not a Novel*
Khanga, Yelena	*Soul to Soul: A Black Russian American Family*
Kovic, Ron	*Born on the Fourth of July*
Lovell, Mary S.	*Sound of Wings: The Biography of Amelia Earhart*
McCullough, David	*Truman*
Massie, Robert K.	*Nicholas and Alexandra*
Mehta, Ved	*Sound Shadows of the New World*
Menchu, Rigoberta	*I, Rigoberta Menchu: An Indian Woman in Guatemala*
Mills, Kay	*This Little Light of Mine: The Life of Fannie Lou Hamer*
Milton, Joyce	*Loss of Eden: A Biography of Charles and Anne Morrow Lindbergh*
Moody, Anne	*Coming of Age in Mississippi: An Autobiography*
Mowat, Farley	*Woman in the Mists: The Story of Dian Fossey and the Mountain Gorillas of Africa*
Simon, Kate	*Bronx Primitive: Portraits in a Childhood*

Steffan, Joseph | *Honor Bound: A Gay American Fights for the Right to Serve His Country*

Wolff, Tobias | *This Boy's Life: A Memoir*

Wright, Richard | *Black Boy: A Record of Childhood and Youth*

X, Malcolm | *Autobiography of Malcolm X*

1994 □ DANCE

Anderson, Jack | *Ballet and Modern Dance: A Concise History*

Balanchine, George, and Francis Mason | *101 Stories of the Great Ballets*

Bland, Alexander, and John Percival | *Men Dancing: Performers and Performances*

Gruen, John | *People Who Dance: Twenty-two Dancers Tell Their Own Stories*

Haskins, James | *Black Dance in America: A History through Its People*

Jonas, Gerald | *Dancing: The Pleasure, Power, and Art of Movement*

Kendall, Elizabeth | *Where She Danced: The Birth of American Art Dance*

Kerner, Mary | *Barefoot to Balanchine: How to Watch Dance*

Tharp, Twyla | *Push Comes to Shove*

Villella, Edward | *Prodigal Son: Dancing for Balanchine in a World of Pain and Magic*

1994 □ FICTION

Achebe, Chinua | *Things Fall Apart*

Alvarez, Julia | *How the Garcia Girls Lost Their Accents*

Austen, Jane | *Pride and Prejudice*

Avi | *Nothing but the Truth*

Bradbury, Ray | *Fahrenheit 451*

Brontë, Charlotte | *Jane Eyre*

Camus, Albert | *Stranger*

Cormier, Robert | *Chocolate War*

Dickens, Charles	*Great Expectations*
Dorris, Michael	*Yellow Raft on Blue Water*
Esquivel, Laura	*Like Water for Chocolate*
Faulkner, William	*Portable Faulkner*
Fitzgerald, F. Scott	*Great Gatsby*
Gaines, Ernest J.	*Autobiography of Miss Jane Pittman*
Gaines, Ernest J.	*Gathering of Old Men*
Golding, William	*Lord of the Flies*
Hemingway, Ernest	*Old Man and the Sea*
Hesse, Hermann	*Siddhartha*
Kingsolver, Barbara	*Animal Dreams: A Novel*
Lee, Gus	*China Boy*
Lee, Harper	*To Kill a Mockingbird*
McCullers, Carson	*Member of the Wedding*
McKinley, Robin	*Beauty*
Morrison, Toni	*Bluest Eye*
Mowry, Jess	*Way past Cool: A Novel*
Orwell, George	*Animal Farm*
Paton, Alan	*Cry, the Beloved Country*
Poe, Edgar Allan	*Selected Tales*
Potok, Chaim	*Chosen*
Salinger, J. D.	*Catcher in the Rye*
Shaara, Michael	*Killer Angels*
Smiley, Jane	*Ordinary Love; and Good Will: Two Novellas*
Solzhenitsyn, Alexander	*One Day in the Life of Ivan Denisovich*
Steinbeck, John	*Of Mice and Men*
Tan, Amy	*Joy Luck Club*
Tolkien, J. R. R.	*Lord of the Rings*
Twain, Mark	*Adventures of Huckleberry Finn*
Uchida, Yoshiko	*Picture Bride*
Vonnegut, Kurt	*Slaughterhouse Five; or, The Children's Crusade*
Walker, Alice	*Color Purple*

1994 □ FILM

Bogle, Donald

Toms, Coons, Mulattoes, Mammies and Bucks: An Interpretative History of Blacks in American Films

Brownlow, Kevin

Hollywood: The Pioneers

Fraser, George M.

Hollywood History of the World: From One Million Years B.C. to Apocalypse Now

Jones, Chuck

Chuck Amuck: The Life and Times of an Animated Cartoonist

Springer, John Shipman

They Sang! They Danced! They Romanced!: A Pictorial History of the Movie Musical

Winship, Michael

Television

1994 □ MUSIC

Allen, Ray

Singing in the Spirit: African American Sacred Quartets in New York City

Bernstein, Leonard

Joy of Music

Boyd, Jenny

Musicians in Tune: Seventy-five Contemporary Musicians Discuss the Creative Process

Kogan, Judith

Nothing but the Best: The Struggle for Perfection at the Juilliard School

Malone, Bill C.

Country Music U.S.A.

Newquist, H. P.

Music and Technology

Sidran, Ben

Talking Jazz: An Illustrated Oral History

Sweeny, Philip

Virgin Directory of World Music

Zeitz, Petra

Rock Star Interviews: Conversations with Leading Performers and Songwriters

1994 □ NONFICTION

Adams, Douglas, and Mark Cowardine

Last Chance to See

Angell, Roger

Season Ticket: A Baseball Companion

Asinoff, Eliot	*Eight Men Out: The Black Sox and the 1919 World Series*
Attenborough, David	*Living Planet: A Portrait of the Earth*
Baldwin, James	*Fire Next Time*
Bell, Eric T.	*Men of Mathematics*
Bernstein, Carl, and Bob Woodward	*All the President's Men*
Boston Women's Health Book Collective Staff	*The New Our Bodies, Ourselves*
Brown, Dee	*Bury My Heart at Wounded Knee: An Indian History of the American West*
Burrough, Bryan, and John Helyar	*Barbarians at the Gate: The Fall of RJR Nabisco*
Campbell, Joseph	*Power of Myth*
Carson, Rachel	*Silent Spring*
Clarke, Arthur C.	*How the World Was One: Beyond the Global Village*
Cleaver, Eldridge	*Soul on Ice*
Dorris, Michael	*Broken Cord*
Du Bois, W. E. B.	*Souls of Black Folk: Essays and Sketches*
Edelman, Marian Wright	*Measure of Our Success: A Letter to My Children and Yours*
Embury, Barbara, with Thomas D. Crouch	*Dream Is Alive*
Epstein, Norrie	*Friendly Shakespeare: A Thoroughly Painless Guide to the Best of the Bard*
Evans, Eli	*Lonely Days Were Sundays: Reflections of a Jewish Southerner*
Faludi, Susan	*Backlash: The Undeclared War against American Women*
Freedman, Samuel C.	*Small Victories: The Real World of a Teacher, Her Students, and Their High School*
Gleick, James	*Chaos: Making a New Science*
Gould, Stephen Jay	*Bully for Brontosaurus: Reflections in Natural History*
Halberstam, David	*Best and the Brightest*

Hawking, Stephen W.	*Brief History of Time: From the Big Bang to Black Holes*
Hersey, John	*Hiroshima*
Hong, Maria (ed.)	*Growing Up Asian American: An Anthology*
Jung, Carl Gustav	*Man and His Symbols*
Karlsen, Carol F.	*Devil in the Shape of a Woman: Witchcraft in Colonial New England*
Karnow, Stanley	*Vietnam: A History*
Kaysen, Susanna	*Girl, Interrupted*
Knaefler, Tomi Kaizawa	*Our House Divided: Seven Japanese American Families in World War II*
Kotlowitz, Alex	*There Are No Children Here: The Story of Two Boys Growing Up in the Other America*
Kozol, Jonathan	*Savage Inequalities: Children in America's Schools*
Lederer, Richard	*Miracle of Language*
Leopold, Aldo	*Sand County Almanac*
Lewis, Anthony	*Gideon's Trumpet*
McCullough, David	*Johnstown Flood*
McPhee, John	*Control of Nature*
McPherson, James M.	*Battle Cry of Freedom: The Civil War Era*
Manley, Deborah (ed.)	*Guinness Book of Records 1492: The World Five Hundred Years Ago*
Maybury-Lewis, Davi	*Millennium: Tribal Wisdom and the Modern World*
Meltzer, Milton	*Rescue: The Story of How Gentiles Saved Jews in the Holocaust*
Mintz, Steven, and Susan Kellogg	*Domestic Revolutions: A Social History of Domestic Family Life*
Nabhan, Gary Paul	*Desert Smells like Rain: A Naturalist in Papago Indian Country*
Northrup, Solomon	*Twelve Years a Slave*
Quindlen, Anna	*Thinking Out Loud: On the Personal, the Political, the Public, and the Private*
Raghaven, Iyer (ed.)	*Essential Writings of Mahatma Gandhi*
Robinette, Diane	*Hometown Heroes: Successful Deaf Youth in America*

Rodriguez, Luis

Always Running: La Vida Loca, Gang Days in L.A.

Rogosin, Donn

Invisible Men: Life in Baseball's Negro Leagues

Sergios, Paul

One Boy at War: My Life in the AIDS Underground

Sheehan, Neil

Bright Shining Lie: John Paul Vann and America in Vietnam

Shenkman, Richard

Legends, Lies, and Cherished Myths of World History

Shilts, Randy

Conduct Unbecoming: Gays and Lesbians in the U.S. Military

Spiegelman, Art

Maus: A Survivor's Tale

Spiegelman, Art

Maus II: Here My Troubles Began

Terkel, Studs

Race: How Blacks and Whites Think and Feel about the American Obsession

Terkel, Susan Neiburg

Should Drugs Be Legalized?

Thomas, Lewis

Youngest Science: Notes of a Medicine Watcher

Tuchman, Barbara Wertheim

Distant Mirror: The Calamitous Fourteenth Century

U.S. Holocaust Museum

World Must Know: The History of the Holocaust as Told in the United States Holocaust Memorial Museum

Vare, Ethlie A., and Greg Ptacek

Mothers of Invention: From the Bra to the Bomb: Forgotten Women and Their Unforgettable Ideas

Walker, Alice

Living by the Word: Selected Writings 1973–1987

Wallis, Velma

Two Old Women: An Alaska Legend of Betrayal, Courage and Survival

Weiss, Ann E.

Who's to Know? Information, the Media and Public Awareness

Williams, Juan

Eyes on the Prize: America's Civil Rights Years 1954–1965

Yolen, Jane (ed.)

Favorite Folktales from Around the World

1994 □ POETRY

Heaney, Seamus, and Ted Hughes (eds.)	*Rattle Bag*
Koch, Kenneth, and Kate Farrell	*Sleeping on the Wing: An Anthology of Modern Poetry, with Essays on Reading and Writing*
Luce, William	*Belle of Amherst*
McClatchy, J. D. (ed.)	*Vintage Book of Contemporary American Poetry*
Pack, Robert, and Jay Parini (eds.)	*Poems for a Small Planet: Contemporary American Nature Poetry*
Soto, Gary	*Fire in My Hands: A Book of Poems*

1994 □ RELATED ARTS

Blackstone Jr., Harry	*Blackstone Book of Magic and Illusion*
Reidelbach, Maria	*Completely Mad: A History of the Comic Books and Magazine*
Spandorfer, Merle	*Making Art Safely: Alternative Methods and Materials in Drawings, Paintings, Printmaking, Graphic Design and Photography*

1994 □ THEATER

Aristophanes	*Lysistrata*
Bernstein, Leonard	*West Side Story*
Brecht, Bertolt	*Mother Courage and Her Children: A Chronicle of the Thirty Years War*
Brockett, Oscar G.	*History of the Theatre*
Christie, Agatha	*Mousetrap*
Cooper, Susan, and Hume Cronyn	*Foxfire*
Coroson, Richard	*Stage Makeup*
Coward, Noel	*Blithe Spirit*
Damashek, Barbara	*Quilters*
Davis, Ossie	*Purlie Victorious: A Commemorative*
Fierstein, Harvey	*Torch Song Trilogy: Three Plays*

Fugard, Athol	*Master Harold and the Boys*
Fuller, Charles	*Soldier's Play: A Play*
Gardner, Herb	*I'm Not Rappaport*
Gottfried, Martin	*Sondheim*
Griffin, Tom	*Boys Next Door: A Play in Two Acts*
Hecht, Ben, and Charles MacArthur	*Front Page*
Hellman, Lillian	*Children's Hour*
Henderson, Mary C.	*Theatre in America: Two Hundred Years of Plays, Players and Productions*
Henley, Beth	*Crimes of the Heart*
Herman, Jerry, and Michael Stewart	*Hello, Dolly!*
Hwang, David Henry	*M. Butterfly*
Ibsen, Henrik	*Doll's House*
Ionesco, Eugene	*Rhinoceros*
John, Errol	*Moon on a Rainbow Shawl; a Play in Three Acts*
Jones, James Earl	*James Earl Jones: Voices and Silences*
Jones, Tom	*Fantasticks*
Kushner, Tony	*Angels in America: Millenium Approaches; Perestroika*
Lawrence, Jerome, and Robert E. Lee	*Inherit the Wind*
Lounsbury, Warren	*Theatre Backstage from A to Z*
Mantle, Burns	*The Best Plays of . . .*
Marsolais, Kenneth, Rodger McFarlane, and Tom Viola	*Broadway, Day and Night*
Medoff, Mark	*Children of a Lesser God*
Miller, Arthur	*Playing for Time: A Screenplay*
Molière, Jean	*Miser*
O'Neill, Eugene	*Ah, Wilderness!*
Perry, George	*Complete Phantom of the Opera*
Pinter, Harold	*Betrayal*
Rodgers, Richard, and Oscar Hammerstein	*Oklahoma!*
Schonberg, Claude-Michel	*Les Miserables*
Shakespeare, William	*Romeo and Juliet*

Shange, Ntozake	*For Colored Girls Who Have Considered Suicide, When the Rainbow Is Enuf*
Shaw, George Bernard	*Pygmalion*
Shepard, Sam	*Buried Child and Seduced and Suicide in B-Flat*
Shue, Larry	*Foreigner*
Simon, Neil	*Lost in Yonkers*
Sondheim, Stephen, and James Lapine	*Into the Woods*
Stoppard, Tom	*Rosencrantz and Guildenstern Are Dead*
Sullivan, Arthur	*Pirates of Penzance*
Walcott, Derek	*Dream on Monkey Mountain, and Other Plays*
Wasserstein, Wendy	*Heidi Chronicles*
Webber, Andrew Lloyd	*Cats*
Wilde, Oscar	*Importance of Being Earnest*
Wilder, Thornton	*Matchmaker*
Williams, Tennessee	*Glass Menagerie*
Wilson, August	*Fences: A Play*
Wilson, August	*Piano Lesson*

APPENDIX

Guidelines for Outstanding Books

for the College Bound Committee

Charge

To prepare a revised and updated edition of the *Outstanding Books for the College Bound* booklists, last published in 1991.

Purpose

To provide reading recommendations to students who plan to continue their education beyond high school.

Audience

The lists are primarily intended for students in grades 9–12 who wish to enrich and strengthen their knowledge in various subject areas of both classic and contemporary literature.

The lists can be used by students who wish to round out their reading before entering college, as well as those taking college entrance examinations such as the ACT and SAT.

The lists can also be used by young adults and adults who are lifelong learners and wish to increase or update their knowledge of literature in the areas covered by the lists.

Eligibility

All books published in English

Books can be in print or out of print

Books that have appeared on earlier "Outstanding Books" lists

Revised editions of books that have appeared on earlier "Outstanding Books" lists

Books that fit into each category (biography, fiction, fine arts, nonfiction, and theater) as defined by the committee.

Voting Procedures

Each committee will determine their own voting procedures. (Selection committees use a variety of voting procedures; however, most of them use a simple or a two-thirds majority for the final vote.)

Recommended Selection Procedures

- Determine criteria for selection

- Standard selection criteria consonant with the ALA Library Bill of Rights shall be applied

- Review titles on the 1991 lists

- Survey other lists of recommended books. Some examples are:
    Good Reading. 23rd ed. Bowker, 1990
    Books for You. 11th ed. NCTE, 1992
    Standard Catalog for High Schools. H. W. Wilson, 1992

- *Best Books for Young Adults.* 1990–1994 ed. ALA

- Bibliographies from specific subject areas

- Current reviews

- Annual lists of outstanding and notable books

- Construct a working list of possible titles during the year for reading, consideration, and examination by the committee

- Choose 40–50 titles for the final list

- Using "Procedures for Writing and Publishing Annotations," determine bibliographic information needed and style required for annotations

- Locate essential bibliographic information according to the "Procedures for Writing and Publishing Annotations" and verify information about author's name, title, and publisher's name

- Write annotations that will appeal to young adults

- Turn in to the OBCB Coordinator by the end of the 1994 Annual Conference a completed list of "Outstanding Books" for your category in hard copy and disk format. If not in IBM WordPerfect, convert to ASCII

AUTHOR INDEX

TITLE INDEX

Before her retirement, Marjorie Lewis was the librarian at Scarsdale (N. Y.) Junior High School for fifteen years. She has been a member of the American Library Association and the Young Adult Library Services Association for almost twenty years, and has served on the Best Books for Young Adults Committee, Genre Committees, Outstanding Books for the College Bound Committee, and the Margaret A. Edwards Award Committee. Lewis is the author of three children's books and a poetry anthology for young women.